CP

000002104580

D1625929

THE WAR HORSES

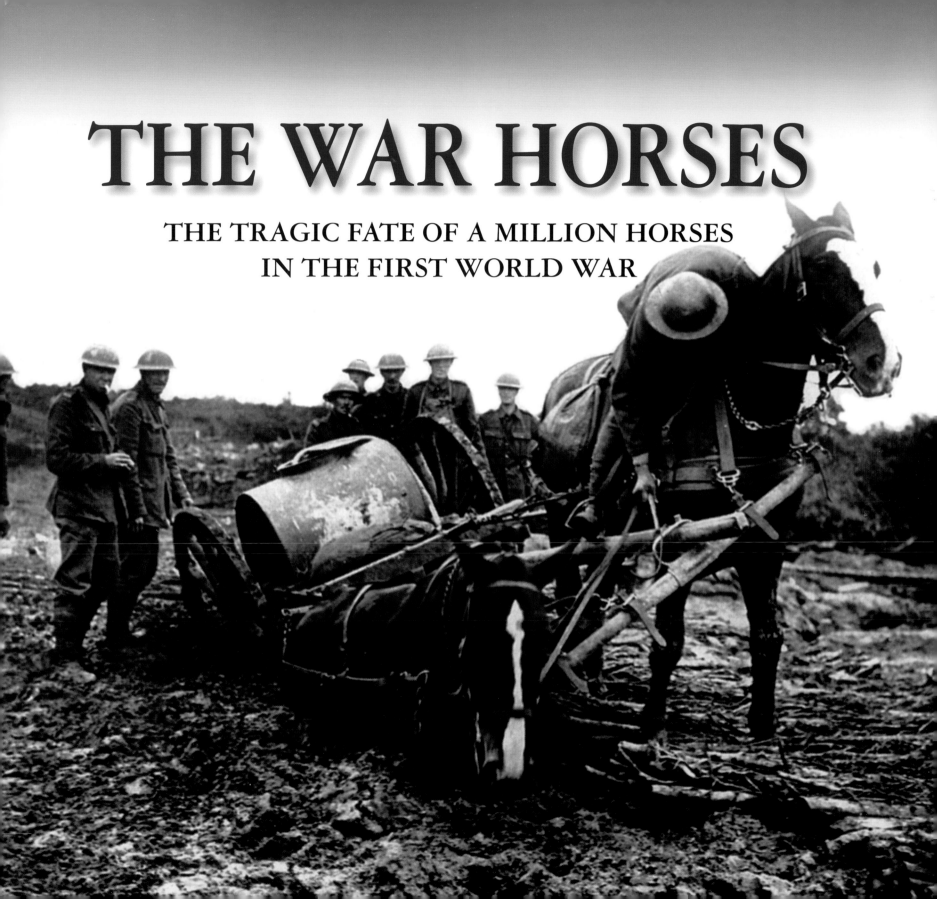

THE WAR HORSES

THE TRAGIC FATE OF A MILLION HORSES
IN THE FIRST WORLD WAR

First published in Great Britain in 2011, reprinted September 2011

Copyright © Simon Butler 2011

British Library Cataloguing-in-Publication Data
A CIP record for this title is available from the British Library

ISBN 978 0 85704 084 8

HALSGROVE
Halsgrove House,
Ryelands Business Park,
Bagley Road, Wellington, Somerset TA21 9PZ
Tel: 01823 653777   Fax: 01823 216796
email: sales@halsgrove.com

Part of the Halsgrove group of companies
Information on all Halsgrove titles is available at: www.halsgrove.com

Printed and bound in China by Everbest Printing Co Ltd

Contents

DEDICATION

*for Anna
and our friends in The Valley*

Foreword

GENERAL SIR FRANK KITSON, GBE, KCB, MC* DL

Simon Butler's book first describes the contribution made by horses to this country in the years leading up to the Great War, showing how greatly the people depended on them for their own movement, the handling of all forms of merchandise and of course for farming. This is followed by a brief account of the way in which horses have been used in wars from the time of Alexander the Great onwards. The book then warms to its main theme, which concerns the part horses played in the operations of the British Army in France between 1914–1918.

The War Horses contains many facts and figures designed to illustrate the variety and importance of the tasks carried out by horses and mules. In this respect the emphasis is rightly given to the bringing up of ammunition and supplies to the front line, the movement of the artillery and the evacuation of casualties. There was little opportunity for the use of cavalry in its traditional role, although some commanders expected that their day would come when the enemy's line was finally breached. None the less, the vast number of horses and mules employed by the British Army was staggering and the extent of the casualties suffered by them, awful. Apparently no less than 256 000 were killed on the Western Front during the war.

But the heart of the book lies beyond the recording of mere facts, as the author depicts the ghastly conditions under which the horses were obliged to live and work and the hardship, terror and appalling pain which they were sometimes obliged to endure. He also describes in touching terms, the feelings of the men as they watched their equine friends struggling against these fearful conditions. A large number of very telling picture emphasise the text.

Although I have read a great number of books about all sorts of war, I have never before been confronted by so vivid an account of its affect on animals. As a person who has enjoyed the company of many horses over the years, I thank heaven that I have never had to take one to war.

Acknowledgements

Thanks are due to those who have inspired and encouraged me in the writing of this book, foremost my family and friends, and particularly Mairi and Tom Hunt, and General Sir Frank Kitson and Lady Kitson; also to everyone at Halsgrove who have supported this project from the outset.

Most of the photographs come from the author's personal collection, and from contemporary books and periodicals, while others have been generously provided by the Hunt family, by Sue Wright whose book on the Norfolk photographer Tom Nokes is soon to be published, and by Barbara Pilch, while others have appeared in volumes of the Halsgrove Community History Series. Author and noted historian Neil Storey gave help in identifying military units appearing in photographs. The main source of official war photographs is the The Haig Papers, part of National Library of Scotland collection, which includes approximately 4000 official war photographs taken from 1916 onwards: Alison Metcalf, Manuscripts Curator was of great help in securing these photographs for use here.

Grateful acknowledgement is made to authors Alison Downes and Alan Childs for references to Jack Juby taken from their book *My Life With Horses*. Other references appear in the select bibliography at the end of this book. No author can ignore the vast resource provided by the internet, with information appearing almost endless as far as the First World War is concerned, leading inevitably to a degree of conflict regarding facts. For the purposes of this book I have stuck to official sources, public records, parliamentary reports and War Office Cabinet minutes wherever possible. There are a number of diaries and memoirs that I have referred to, in particular the diary of Travis Hampton MC, whose family I have attempted to trace without success. Should they or any other individuals wish to contact me I would be happy to make the necessary acknowledgements in future editions of this work.

Preface

This book grew out of a chance conversation with horse-woman and sculptor Mairi Laing Hunt whose sculptural works in bronze include superb equestrian pieces. I, being a non-horse person (although I have the good fortune that horses appear to like me), was intrigued to learn more of what drew people to horses and of that particular relationship that certain individuals have with the horse.

As part of our conversation Mairi told me about her grandparents, the Paisley family, who had, before the First World War, run a successful livery and stables in Harrogate. At the outbreak of the war, like so many others, the family had been obliged to part with the best of their mounts under the requisition orders which allowed the British government to select horses for war work. As the animals were taken from the stable yard, Mrs Paisley would attach to their bridles a piece of cloth on which the name of the horse was written. She well knew that each animal responded to its own name. Years later, a cavalry officer told her how much the naming of each animal had meant to the men who were given charge of the horses under military command.

An officer and men of the Westmoreland and Cumberland Yeomanry, a cavalry regiment, at camp in England c.1914. The regiment remained in England during the first years of the war, sailing for France in 1917 to fight in the trenches as dismounted troops; a common fate among many erstwhile mounted units.

Captain Tom Paisley, sitting on the bale of hay, joined up shortly after the outbreak of war in 1914. Earlier, his family had given up horses from their livery and stables in Harrogate, Yorkshire, for use by the British Army. Note the corn crusher (centre) used to prepare grain such as oats for horse feed, and the chaff cutter (left) used for cutting hay into smaller pieces before being fed to horses.

At the sharp end of the conflict only the most insensitive of fighting men could have ignored the plight of these beasts as they were subjected to the most trying conditions of the battlefield. And on the Home Front too the consequences of the war brought heartache, as a young Elizabeth Owen recalled:

> Then we heard that the khaki men were coming to take away all the horses from the village. Everything in the village was done by horses. The station was about a mile or a mile and a half away and the train was met by a brake drawn by horses. The milk was delivered by horses and the butter used to be collected from the farms and brought in by horses to the butter market. There was a farmer who had a lovely pair who we called the prancers. He thought he would try and hide these horses but the khaki men found them. They tied them all together on a long rope, I think there was about twenty – all horses we used to know and love and feed. Then they started trotting them out of the village and as they went out of sight we were all terribly sad.

Within the story of the horse at war, this book illustrates how people who know and work with horses respond instinctively to the bonds that tie these sensitive beasts to the will of man; a bond that springs from deep within the well of human history. The war of 1914–18 was the first and last global conflict in which the horse played a vital role. It was also the point at which the relationship between humans and horses could be said to have changed forever.

Simon Butler
Manaton 2011

Introduction

It is estimated that ten million fighting men, over 800 000 of them British, died in the First World War. Only a fraction of those who were killed have a known grave – thousands were simply blown into fragments or lie buried, their graves unknown, in foreign soil. In the decades following the war's end hundreds of books appeared written by soldiers, politicians, poets and preachers, each trying to make sense of the conflict, the appalling conditions and the seemingly pointless slaughter. No other war has produced so much literature, a poet in every platoon it seems, producing a huge range of work from Rupert Brooke's idealistic sonnets through to the plaintive, and truer, voices of Wilfred Owen and Siegfried Sassoon. Even today, almost a century on, novelists look to the First World War as a backdrop in which grief and hopelessness strike an immediate chord with their readers. Simply put, the Great War has become a metaphor for hell on earth.

Early in the war, men in Britain were volunteering to get to the front, stirred by jingoism and patriotic fervour (only later was conscription needed to replace the slaughtered legions who would never come home). Alongside this tide of human cannon-fodder was formed an army of horses and mules, transport essential to the bloody business ahead. While men volunteered in their tens of thousands, similar numbers of horses were being stripped from farms, liveries, hunt stables and from private ownership, to be shipped abroad. This book tells some of the story of the part these animals played in the war itself, and of the consequences of the conflict which led to the decline of horses in the British landscape and the final fracturing of a timeless bond between man and horse.

While the study of the fate of men who fought in the First World War has reached industrial proportions in books and film, much less is known of the fate of the horses in that conflict. Essential to the movement of troops and heavy equipment, many of these animals were removed under government orders from quiet rural farms and sent into the heat of battle.

Over a million horses died during the war on the Western Front alone on the Allied side. Of the million or so animals listed as being in service with the British and Commonwealth forces (excluding other Allied forces) during the course of the war, some authorities suggest only 60 000 were returned to Britain after the war's end.

As Secretary of State for War in 1914, Field Marshal Herbert Kitchener was responsible for organising a volunteer army. Using propaganda such as this leaflet which refers to German atrocities in Belgium, and backed by a concerted promotional campaign 'Your Country Needs You', he raised an army of three million in two years.

This is not a comprehensive study and is largely concerned with the British Army on the Western Front. It concentrates on those groups of animals who were requisitioned rather than those 'professionally' employed by the cavalry, in other words the horses and mules who took on the drudgery of heaving rations, guns and munitions up to the front lines, often returning with wounded and maimed men. It looks at the lives the animals would have known in peacetime, comparing them with the conditions they were thrust into in and around the lines of battle. It draws upon photographs and personal accounts to illustrate the actuality of war and the part played by the horse in the prosecution of that conflict.

The book attempts to draw in a wider theme too, that of the discontinuity of an ancient relationship between man and the natural world, here represented by the horse; a gradual estrangement resultant, in part, from the cataclysm of the Great War.

Winter on the Western Front, 1916. The patient pair of mules hitched to a water cart stand on hard frosted ground while a party of soldiers, muffled against the cold, work to fill old petrol tins with water from a pump outside a ruined building. Bleak scenes such as this would have been played out thousands of time during the 1914–18 war: men and animals working alongside each other in the harshest circumstances.

Horse Power

It is important to remember that our twenty-first century enlightened views on animal welfare, particularly regarding the treatment of horses, differs from that of our predecessors. But our sentimentality should not be confused with sensitivity, and in many ways, due to their dependence on animals both wild and domestic, our forebears had a greater empathy with them. But animals that are primarily bred for work, or for food, being bought and sold in markets, are almost certain to be regarded as 'belongings' rather than sentient beings. Necessity demanded pragmatism among those whose lives depended upon a workhorse performing well for instance, and in times when human life itself was cheap, cruelty to animals was commonplace.

But in the century before the First World War reformers were at work in Britain, and in the 1820s the first anti-cruelty bill was introduced by Richard Martin MP, better known as 'Humanity Dick'. His aim was to reduce the cruel treatment of farm animals – specifically making it an offence to 'wantonly beat, abuse or ill-treat' any 'horse, cow, ox, heifer, steer, sheep or other cattle' – and two years after the Act was passed in 1822, Martin and his supporters created the Society for the Prevention of Cruelty to Animals, the first of its kind in any country, and which became the RSPCA in 1840 after being granted royal status by Queen Victoria.

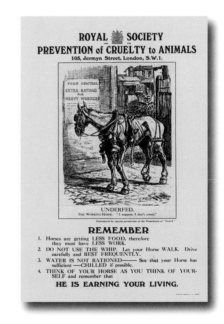

Even as early as 1751 Hogarth had produced his series of engravings 'The Four Stages of Cruelty', the second in the series depicting the villain, Tom Nero, as a hackney cabman, beating his mistreated horse which has fallen and broken its leg, overturning the carriage. The artist's satirical commentary on society, in this case exemplified through cruel acts, was a theme later to be taken up by the poet William Blake who, around 1800, denounced cruelty to animals in mystical terms. 'A horse misused upon the road,' he writes in *Auguries of Innocence*, 'Calls to heaven for human blood'.

An RSPCA poster entreating those who work with horses to 'Think of Your Horse as You Think of Yourself'.

In the Victorian period, popular writers of the day continued the movement towards a more compassionate society through their writings. Charles Dickens in *Oliver Twist* emphasises the notion that cruelty to animals leads to depravity and corruption in humans, with the ill-treatment by the notorious Bill Sikes of his dog Bull's-Eye being a prelude to the murder of the hapless Nancy. But most famous of all such books is Anna Sewell's *Black Beauty* published in 1877. Written in the last years of her life, it became one of the best-selling books of all time, with 50 million copies sold. Through

Anna Sewell's famous novel was the first to arouse in the public popular support for the cause of animal welfare, particularly that of horses.

its main character, the horse after whom the novel is named, the author provides a forthright lesson in animal welfare as well as teaching people how to respect one another. Two of the major characters are Captain, an ex-army mount who survives the Charge of the Light Brigade, and Ginger, a horse damaged by her upbringing and who dies cruelly as a broken-down cab horse.

Stirred by such writers, at the time of the outbreak of the First World War, the British tended to congratulate themselves on their civilised attitude to animal welfare; their pets in particular. On this issue they looked down on the rest of the world. They had become a nation of 'animal-lovers'.

Away from the domestic scene, within city boundaries, horse power remained the dominant means of moving goods and people. That great recorder of metropolitan life, Henry Mayhew, describes the work of Londoners whose occupations are reliant upon horses and donkeys. And here, around the 1850s, the Briton's concern for his animal charges is apparent:

> *The costermongers (street sellers of fish and vegetables etc) almost universally treat their donkeys with kindness. Many a costermonger will resent the ill-treatment of a donkey, as he would a personal indignity. These animals are not only favourites, but pets, having their share of the costermonger's dinner when bread forms a portion of it...'*

Even the cab and omnibus drivers, much ma- ligned in popular fiction for their brutish ways, are redeemed in Mayhew's accounts. Here an omnibus driver discusses his animals' work in sympathetic terms:

> *The starting after stopping is the hardest work for them it's such a terrible strain. I've felt for the poor things on a wet night, with a 'bus full of big people.*

Towards the end of Victoria's reign, the popu- lation of England's major cities were growing rapidly. Transport, whether of goods or people, remained largely dependent upon the horse.

Horse-drawn vehicles of every description vie for space in the crowded streets outside the Bank of England, London c.1900.

The London Cab Driver, an illustration from Mayhew's London *published in 1851.*

In 1900 there were 11 000 horse-drawn cabs in London along with 1000 horse-buses, requiring in excess of 50 000 horses. Additionally there were countless carts, carriages, drays and wains each working from dawn until dusk to deliver goods throughout the metropolis. One correspondent to *The Times* in 1894 estimated that within fifty years every street in London would be buried under nine feet of manure!

But it was on the land that the ancient beliefs and traditions of working with horses survived well into the twentieth century. Indeed a remaining vestige of these beliefs survives even today, though for not much longer perhaps, in the shape of the 'lucky' horseshoe. Its relation to the horse gives the shoe a talismanic value, the horse being revered in ancient cultures and almost certainly into prehistory. British mythology ascribes to the horse the character of a luck-bringer, and horse-worship was practised among the early Celts, Teutons, and Slavs of Europe.

While variations of the cultish practices of working with horses could be found in each county in Britain, many of theses beliefs and customs sprang from the same source. In part these were indeed based on 'magic' – especially in the breeding and training of young animals, and in matters concerning cures when an animal was sick.

It was the chronicler of rural traditions in East Anglia, George Ewart Evans, who perhaps did most to record what remained of these beliefs in the mid twentieth century. Interviews with surviving horsemen appearing in his book *Horse Power and Magic* provide a glimpse of pre-mechanisation on farms when the horse and the horseman's power reigned.

Thomas Sidney Cooper (1803–1902) was an English artist whose lithographs featured farm animals, often cattle and horses. In this scene 'Hay Cart Returning From Market' c.1837 he captures many of the elements associated with working horses in a rural environment. The beasts stand placidly outside an inn, briefly released from the toil of the working day. A donkey laden with panniers rests alongside the wagon's wheel. Artists during this period satisfied a growing public appetite in which the middle classes decorated their homes with scenes portraying rural life as a dying idyll.

True, some of this 'power' arose from the inclination of craftsmen to contain the secrets of their trade within a select band of brothers, and one such was The Society of the Horseman's World, formed in Scotland in the eighteenth century, surviving to the twentieth. Membership involved an initiation ceremony and the taking of oaths from which the initiate, often a ploughboy 'apprentice', would be given the secret 'Word' which thereafter gave them power over horses. Merely whispering the Word would bring the animal under their control. The present-day excitement over 'Horse Whisperers' owes something to these early beliefs.

It is difficult for twenty-first century minds to appreciate that it is only a little over a century since these ideas began to fade. It is certain that many who went to fight in the First World War took with them an inherent belief in the age-old practices associated with horses and their management – knowledge that in itself helped form a bond with the animals which also went to war.

A magnificent specimen, the Clydesdale 'Laura Lee', foaled in 1884. Such heavy horses were the principal form of motive power on farms for generations. As Edward Hart records in his book The Suffolk Punch:

'If you lived in the country as I do, you would sometimes see a sight that would make your blood run cold, and yet it is so common a sight that we country people grow accustomed to it. You would see a great lumbering tumbril, weighing a ton or two with two wheels nearly six feet high, loaded with manure, drawn by a great Suffolk cart-horse as big as an elephant, and conducted by a tiny thing of a boy who can scarcely reach the horse's nose to take hold of the rein.'

One of the last surviving horsemen, born as the First World War ended but brought up in the mystique of these earlier traditions, was the celebrated East Anglian, Jack Juby. His name was without peer in the world of heavy horses, particularly the Suffolk Punch, right up to his death in 2004. In his reminiscences, included in the biography *My Life With Horses,* there are constant echoes of the ancient practises and beliefs. The book includes a photograph of Jack's 'secret book' said to contain 'the accumulated wisdom of generations passed down from Horseman to Horseman'. One recipe the handwritten book contains is intriguingly titled 'How to Manage a Vicious Horse so as to be able to do anything with him'.

During his lifetime Jack Juby was witness to the transition from the almost exclusive use of horse power to total mechanical power on farms in Britain. One day whilst travelling through Norfolk, Jack stopped to admire some Percherons standing in a field when a local passed by on his bike. 'Hello Jack, what are you doing about here? You want to tell your governor to come and buy those horses. She's packing up. She isn't going to breed any more 'cos tractors are getting about.'

A horse-drawn sledge in use at Foxworthy on Dartmoor c.1880. On rough, uneven and muddy ground the sledge was more effective than a wheeled vehicle, and as a conveyance the sledge remained in use throughout the First World War (see page 61).

"Carriage of every kind was done entirely on the backs of horses; except in harvest, when sledges were sometimes used. Twenty years ago there was not a pair of wheels in-country, at least not on a farm."

William Marshall (writing about Dartmoor), 1796

Croft breaking near Nancegollan in Cornwall around 1900. The unbroken ground was so hard it took many horses to pull the plough.

Farm labourers and their horse at Foxworthy in the 1880s. Here a rest is taken from the arduous work of raking and burning the turf, preparing the field for sowing.

"The hours of work are well regulated. The plowteams make two journeys a day: they go out before eight in the morning, and return at twelve. Go out again before two, and return before six: working about eight hours a day."

William Marshall, 1796

Ploughing at Foxworthy c.1910

The heavy horse breeds familiar to Jack Juby, including the Percherons, Suffolks, Clydesdales and Shires, dwindled to the point of extinction as their use on farms declined; the Suffolk Punch being listed as an endangered species. Ewart Evans remarks on the changes: 'Before the coming of mechanical power John Goddard needed thirty horses to work his land. But he wanted more power and he was one of the first to experiment with old steam ploughs'. Goddard invested in an early steam plough made by Garrets of Leiston and ironically called 'The Suffolk Punch', but he later scrapped it and went back to horse power for a while, then on to motor tractors.

Threshing corn using a steam traction engine c.1890. Both the 'thrashing' machine and the elevator are driven by the engine. Though the number of men required for labour is considerable, the process would be much quicker than using horse power alone.

The early use of steam engines on farms, introduced in the early 1800s, was limited due to the enormous weight of these thunderous machines which simply got bogged down on soft ground. Only with the development of the high-pressure boiler which allowed for much lighter engines did the farmer see steam as a viable option to horse power. Even then its use was limited to those who could buy machines of their own, or afford to make use of contractors. Between 1850 and 1914, steam power gradually grew in use and where once the

A steam plough operating on a Suffolk farm. Two of these machines would operate together, sited at each end of the field to be ploughed. Tethered by the huge winch seen beneath this engine, the plough would be hauled across the field between one machine and the other, creeping forward in unison as each furrow was completed. Few farms could afford to own their own machinery and these plough sets moved from farm to farm under contract.

countryside rang to the sound of horses hooves and the encouraging shouts of the horsemen, now clouds of smoke billowed from the stacks of lumbering mechanical engines that rattled and clanked on their way to the fields.

But by no means was the introduction of these machines seen as universally bad. Indeed, most of those who laboured in the fields welcomed the respite they gave from back-breaking tasks such as ploughing, threshing, mowing with scythes, planting and gathering of root crops. Nor did the appearance of these machines spell the end of horse power. Most small farms, and those in upland areas on terrain where these huge and heavy machines were difficult to operate, clung on to the old ways for many decades into the twentieth century. Besides which, compared to the horse, steam engines were difficult and dangerous to operate, expensive to buy and maintain.

But even as Victoria's long reign came to an end, the writing was on the wall for horse power in the countryside. Younger men were drawn to the excitement of driving these new beasts, and farmers were seeking ways to reduce labour costs at the same time as increasing yields of crops to feed the millions now moving to live in cities.

Along with making ironwork and shoeing horses the village blacksmith found himself turning his hand to repairing leaking boilers and broken gears as steam engines appeared more regularly in the countryside.

21

Contrasting scenes on farms before the First World War. Both photographs were taken c.1910, the one opposite on Foxworthy Farm on Dartmoor and the one below at a farm in Norfolk. In previous centuries the limits placed on farming by the available use of power, i.e. the horse, meant that most farms, particularly in upland areas, were relatively small. While the work was hard and subject to the variations of the seasons, life itself was one-paced – in equine terms a walk rather than a trot.

The advent of machinery was generally welcomed by farm labourers, providing as it did respite from heavy, time-consuming and onerous tasks such as threshing. The poses adopted by the figures in this scene at Blofield, Norfolk, is some indication of the novelty generated by the arrival of a steam engine.

HORSE POWER

The growth of railways made it possible to transport even the most perishable goods to these new urban markets, with milk and vegetables being sent daily from the farther reaches of the British Isles. For a time at least, horse transport remained important in getting goods and people to and from the railway stations, and as a general means of transportation. At the same time the number of horses in agriculture in England and Wales increased marginally between the mid 1800s and the end of the century when the total stood at around 1.3 million. But motor cars were already growing in popularity and in 1896 the Red Flag Act was withdrawn giving the motorist freedom of the open road. By 1900 there were 10 000 cars in Britain, the majority privately owned.

Yet despite the numbers of motor vehicles appearing on roads in the first decade of the twentieth century most haulage of goods and people was still done by horses. Mechanical transport was costly to buy, costly to run, and difficult to maintain. Farmers owned tried-and-tested wagons, ploughs, binders, seed drills, harrows and rakes, all horse-drawn, and had the men who were used to working with horses (and whose wages were poor). Animals could be fed by hay and oats that were grown on the farm and thus were self-sufficient in their care. There was a reluctance to change.

And for these reasons the horse remained a primary means of motive power. Even the power of the steam engine and, later, the motor-car, continued to be measured against that of the horse. In 1906 Rolls Royce introduced the prestigious Silver Ghost, the four-cylinder version being designated 30HP. In and around cities the improvement in road surfaces encouraged the movement towards mechanical transport, while rural areas kept faith with the horse.

Horse-drawn wagons belonging to the Great Western Railway loaded with blankets bound for London. Up to the First World War most freight was carried to and from the railhead by horses.

THE WAR HORSES

From ponies running the family in the jingle to chapel on Sundays, to quarry teams hauling vast loads, man's centuries-old relationship with the horse remained strong The huntsmen and women maintained their social status at weekly meets in the grounds of country estates, riding high on thoroughbreds, while horse-racing 'the sport of kings' had never been more popular.

Wars, for the Victorians and Edwardians, where they had impinged at all upon the life of the British at home, had always been distant enough not to be too troublesome. The Royal Navy kept her enemies at arm's length and in an appropriate state of fear so far as the Empire was concerned. Ironically, at the turn of the century, the one organisation that was deficient in its use and procurement of horses was the British Army which, as the prospect of a European war grew more distinct, had learned little from earlier conflicts as to the numbers of animals it might require, and knew even less regarding the practical uses of horses in modern warfare.

A huge baulk of timber being moved from the railway station at Bakewell, Derbyshire, to a nearby timber yard.

A Kingdom for A Horse

Along with the popular appeal of horses, and that founded on the relationship of the farm worker and his charges, there is a universal human response toward the horse as a symbol of rank, of social standing and especially of military power. It is worth reflecting on this briefly as it once heavily coloured the western view of how battles should be fought and the place of the horse in them.

The horse in battle has an ancient history, dating from the time in which they were first domesticated. In Britain we have Julius Caeser's account of his first expedition to these shores in 55BC. In *The Gallic Wars* he provides a graphic description of the British charioteers in action as the Roman forces attempt to land:

Horses were important to the Romans, not only as cavalry in battle, but also symbolically. They sacrificed a horse to the god Mars each October, keeping its tail throughout the winter as a representation of fertility and rebirth.

> *The barbarians knew what the Romans intended. Sending on ahead their cavalry and charioteers – a kind of warrior whom they habitually employ in action – they followed with the rest of their force and attempted to prevent our men from disembarking. It was very difficult to land, for these reasons. The size of the ships made it impossible for them to ground except in deep water; the soldiers did not know the ground, and with their hands loaded, and weighted by their heavy, cumbrous armour, they had to jump down from the ships, keep their foothold in the surf, and fight the enemy all at once; while the enemy had all their limbs free, they knew the ground perfectly, and standing on dry land or moving forward a little into the water, they threw their missiles boldly and drove their horses into the sea, which they were trained to enter. Our men were unnerved by the situation; and having no experience of this kind of warfare, they did not show the same dash and energy that they generally did in battles on land.*

A few days later, a party of Roman soldiers foraging for food are ambushed. Caesar describes the tactics used by the British horsemen:

> *Chariots are used in action in the following way. First of all the charioteers drive all over the field, the warriors hurling missiles; and generally they throw the enemy's ranks into confusion by the mere terror inspired by their horses and the clatter of the wheels. As soon as they have penetrated between the troops of [their own] cavalry, the warriors jump off the chariots and fight on foot. The drivers meanwhile gradually withdraw from the action, and range the cars in such a position that, if the warriors are hard pressed by the enemy's numbers, they may easily get back to them. Thus they exhibit in action*

Winged victory riding in a chariot.

the mobility of cavalry combined with the steadiness of infantry; and they become so efficient from constant practice and training that they will drive their horses at full gallop, keeping them well in hand, down a steep incline, check and turn them in an instant, run along the pole, stand on the yoke, and step backwards again to the cars with the greatest nimbleness.

From Roman times, despite technological developments, improvements in arms and artillery, the horse played a principal role in most major European wars up to the mid nineteenth century. Even the advent of artillery in the sixteenth century, at first reckoned to spell the end of horse power on the battlefield, actually resulted in an increase in the importance of the horse, especially in the rapid movement of cannon. In 1760 Frederick the Great devised a strategy for quick teams of light horses to pull guns rapidly from point to point during battle – methods later adopted by the British and French armies during the Napoleonic and future wars.

The Duke of Wellington rousing his troops at Waterloo from an oil painting by Robert Alexander Hillingford (1825-1904). The importance of mobile artillery was brought to the fore in the battle.

But it was the Crimean War that proved to be the watershed as far as the British Army's procurement and use of horses was concerned. Breaking out in 1854 and fought over two years it was to some extent to foreshadow the 1914–1918 war in a number of aspects, not least as its cause lay in a clash of interests among European Empires. It was also a war for which the British military was woefully ill-prepared tactically, having failed to grasp the importance of integrating cavalry with artillery and infantry. As a result, the war was to throw up one of the most enduring 'triumphs' of British military history: The Charge of the Light Brigade, immortalised in poetry and paintings.

> *Cannon to right of them,*
> *Cannon to left of them,*
> *Cannon behind them*
> *Volley'd and thunder'd;*
>
> *Storm'd at with shot and shell,*
> *While horse and hero fell,*
> *They that had fought so well*
> *Came thro' the jaws of Death*

Back from the mouth of Hell,
All that was left of them,
Left of six hundred.

Perhaps it is the British genius for moderating disasters into victories, as later in the Zulu Wars at Isandlwana (or rather in the rash of VCs awarded at Rorke's Drift), and at Dunkerque in World War Two, that prevented military minds from learning their lesson in the 'Valley of Death'. It was simple enough: tried and tested cavalry tactics were no longer effective against well placed artillery. The war correspondent William Russell, who witnessed the battle, declared 'our Light Brigade was annihilated by their own rashness, and by the brutality of a ferocious enemy'.

The Charge of the Light Brigade from a painting by Thomas Jones Barker (1815-1882). The Light Brigade under Lord Cardigan had, through mistaken orders, attacked a large Russian force including at least fifty guns. Despite withering fire from three sides that devastated their force on the ride, the Light Brigade was able to engage the Russian forces at the end of the valley and force them back. But having suffered such heavy casualties, it too was soon forced to retire.

It is worthy of note that the Crimean War was the first in which the media had a significant involvement. William Russell of *The Times* sent daily despatches back to his newspaper, via telegraph, which appeared along with artists' impressions of major events the following day. This was the first time that the British public were presented with an immediate commentary on the progress of war. While such reports sensationalised events such as the Charge of the Light Brigade (and brought the work of Florence Nightingale into the public eye), they also had a marked effect on the way in which generals were to conduct this and future wars. In the First World War, for instance, this manifested itself through the General Staff's obsession with 'gaining ground'. Conquering a few yards of territory, often gained at enormous cost in human life, was trumpeted daily in the press.

If the Crimean War had not alerted the generals to the need to rethink their strategy as far as the use of cavalry was concerned, the American Civil War which followed less than a decade later, should have made certain of a lesson worth learning.

A different kind of war. The photograph shows the huge military build-up outside Yorktown, Virginia in 1862, during the American Civil War. Access to the industrial centres of the North and to European arms manufacturers resulted in a proliferation of arms and artillery that turned the battlefields into killing grounds, ultimately creating a static war of set battles and sieges, presaging the trench warfare on the Western Front.

Breaking out in 1861 and lasting until 1865, the Civil War as it unfolded presaged many of the events that were to play out in the First World War. Initially the horse was at the heart of military tactics, providing mobility over long distances in the movement of troops, guns, ammunition and general supplies. Such was its importance that Major General William T. Sherman ordered his troops that 'Every opportunity at a halt during a march should be taken advantage of to cut grass, wheat, or oats and extraordinary care be taken of the horses upon which everything depends'.

At the start of the war, the Northern states held approximately 3.4 million horses, while there were 1.7 million in the Confederate states. The border states of Missouri and Kentucky had an extra 800 000 horses. In addition, there were 100 000 mules in the North, 800 000 in the seceding states and 200 000 in Kentucky and Missouri. During the war, the Union alone used over 825 000 horses and in total it is thought that over a million animals died or were killed.

But as John Keegan points out in his book *The American Civil War*, 'Cavalry simply did not play a decisive or even particularly noticeable role between 1861 and 1865'. Partly this was due to factors such as the distances over which the war raged, partly to the terrain and the lack of a cavalry tradition in the American armed forces. But mainly, and this is the lesson European military commanders failed to learn, it was due to technological developments in weaponry, in artillery, and particularly in the introduction of the rifle and the machine gun. These weapons allowed greater and more effective killing distances between the warring armies, one result of which was the propensity to 'dig in'. Faced with horrendous casualties, with 30 per cent killed and wounded being usual in Civil War battles, it was simply a case of self preservation for the ordinary infantryman to dig a hole whenever possible.

Ultimately it was not one of the great set-piece open battles that might be said to have decided the outcome of the war but a siege more reminiscent of medieval warfare, the attackers investing a city with a circle of guns, the defenders behind fortifications and entrenchments repulsing attacks until starvation forced surrender. This was the siege of Vicksburg, between 25 May and 4 July 1863, following which the Confederates surrendered, yielding command of the vital Mississippi to the Union and splitting the South in two.

Some of the 144 emplaced Civil War cannons that now stand in the Vicksburg National Military Park in Mississippi. It was the proliferation of such weapons, all of course horse-drawn, that led to armies preparing entrenchments, and thus to a more static kind of warfare.

Just five years after the American Civil War ended a new conflict sprang up in Europe. This was the Franco-Prussian War, begun in 1870, and which ended with the unification of Germany. Although Britain was not directly involved, the requirement of the German army for large numbers of horses (they were able to mobilize over a million during the war) led to a government enquiry into how many horses had been exported from Britain to service the war, and whether this had resulted in a shortage at home. The government committee set up to consider the issues indeed discovered an acute shortage of horses for agricultural work, exacerbated by the fact that many farmers had ceased to breed their own equine stock and had, to make matters worse, sold off horses at quick profit to hauliers in the cities.

The hauliers themselves complained about the high cost of purchasing horses, with the London Omnibus Company reporting, in 1872, a rise from an average of £24 to over £32 per head. But the British military authorities, the committee found, seemed even less aware than the haulage business of the more serious problems they might face resulting from a shortage of horses should a war start.

A recruitment poster for the Army Remount Department adds the proviso 'only men thoroughly accustomed to horses need apply'. From 1914 onwards the drain from farms of ploughmen and others used to working with horses became a matter of national concern.

The responsibility of supplying the army with horses fell on the shoulders of the Army Remount Department which originally had two depots, the Remount Establishment at Woolwich, and another in Dublin. The former maintained close links with the artillery and engineers, while the latter depot acted as a centre for the large number of animals that were sourced in Ireland.

By 1887, such was the concern over the supply of horses for the army that a scheme was introduced which allowed owners of horses to register their animals for use by the army in return for a subsidy towards the cost of upkeep, and a guaranteed purchase price in the event of the registered animals being called up in time of war. Two Assistant Inspectors of Remounts were charged with the responsibility of purchasing horses while another handled the registration scheme. In 1891 the Army Service Corps (ASC) took over the responsibility for the depots which were manned by soldiers from cavalry units. Around 1902 two further depots were opened, one at Melton Mowbray, the other at Arborfield in Berkshire.

As will be shown later, the importance of these relatively small units grew substantially from 1914 onwards, although few up to that date could have predicted the enormous numbers of beasts ultimately required.

An idealised view of members of the Army Service Corps in action, from a postcard by the Edgar Alfred Holloway (1870–1941), a noted military artist during the Boer War and the First World War.

Horses and Power and War

Four things greater than all things are,
Women and Horses and Power and War.
Rudyard Kipling
'The Ballad of the King's Jest'

Kipling's verse is worthy of inclusion in the context of this book, at least so far as horses and power and war are concerned. The mythical and cultural symbolism of the horse endured long after its effectiveness in battle had faded, but any lessons that could have been learnt from the Crimea and the American Civil War which might have stood the First World War generals in good stead, were diluted by the lingering notion that cavalry remained the most potent force on the field of battle. More so the fact that cavalry regiments in the British Army maintained a notional position of superiority over the 'poor bloody infantry' giving their officers a greater say in the development of military strategy.

But here we should have some sympathy for the military commanders who stuck to their faith in the cavalry – the power of the horse in the British psyche has never totally diminished. As Winston Churchill, who took part in the last great cavalry charge at Omdurman in 1898, said 'There is something about the outside of a horse that is good for the inside of a man'. And of course Churchill himself, as Home Secretary in 1911 and First Lord of the Admiralty at the outbreak of war in 1914, would have no little influence on the composition of the armed forces. Churchill also served for a brief period on the Western Front having resigned from the government, commanding the 6th Battalion of the Royal Scots Fusiliers.

Long before civilisations developed, prehistoric man drew pictures of horses on cave walls with such care and reverence that one might assume these were far more than pictorial representations. The ancient Greeks worshipped a whole herd of divine steeds, including Pegasus, sired by the immortal horses of the four wind gods which drew the chariot of Zeus.

And one of the most legendary horses of all time could be said to have single-handedly put to an end ten years of otherwise fruitless combat at the walls of the city of Troy. Constructing a wooden horse and hiding thirty men inside, the Greeks then

The charge of the 21st Lancers at the Battle of Omdurman.

'Alexander taming Bucephalus' by the French artist Francois Schommer (1850–1935).

pretended to sail away leaving their Trojan Horse on the shore. Seeing the giant horse as a victory trophy the Trojans pulled it into the city where the hidden force crept out at night to open the gates for the Greek army to enter. What other than a horse, that potent symbol of power in warfare, could have enticed the Trojans to such folly?

Then came Alexander the Great and Bucephalus, not a legendary horse but an actual beast whose prowess in battle has immortalised his name. A huge animal with a black coat and white star, Bucephalus was said to be untamable. King Philip of Macedon refused to buy so wild an animal despite its magnificent breeding, but his son, Alexander, then thirteen, promised to pay for the animal himself should he fail to tame it. Whispering to the horse he turned it toward the sun so that the animal could no longer see its shadow, which had been the cause of its distress, and thus tamed it.

In history, no other pairing of man and horse, has achieved the fame of Alexander and Bucephalus. They fought together in a number of battles, the horse taking on mystic qualities of invincibility. On its death, Alexander – then ruler of the known world – founded a city, Bucepala, (now modern day Jalapur Sharif in Pakistan) named after his faithful warhorse. Such was the power of the stories surrounding the king and his horse, a kind of cult grew up around them and thereafter it was expected that kings and conquerors should have a favourite horse. In *The Lives of the Caesars*, Suetonius describes the chosen mount of Julius Caesar:

He rode a remarkable horse, too, with feet that were almost human; for its hoofs were cloven in such a way as to look like toes. This horse was foaled on his own place, and since the soothsayers had declared that it foretold the rule of the world for its master, he reared it with the greatest care, and was the first to mount it, for it would endure no other rider. Afterwards, too, he dedicated a statue of it before the temple of Venus Genetrix.

French prisoners at the Battle of Agincourt, about to have their throats cut. The loss of so much of France's nobility in the slaughter gave the English endless opportunities to vaunt their success, not least through William Shakespeare who at least had the talent to make unadulterated propaganda exquisitely moving:

> And Crispin Crispian shall ne'er go by,
> From this day to the ending of the world,
> But we in it shall be remembered-
> We few, we happy few, we band of brothers;
> For he to-day that sheds his blood with me
> Shall be my brother; be he ne'er so vile,
> This day shall gentle his condition;
> And gentlemen in England now-a-bed
> Shall think themselves accurs'd they were not here,
> And hold their manhoods cheap whiles any speaks
> That fought with us upon Saint Crispin's day.
>
> Henry V Act 4 Sc 3

A more recent date in history, 25 October 1415, provides a celebrated British victory against massed cavalry – one of the few occasions up to that point when the horse used as a battering ram failed to overcome infantry. Outnumbered at least 5 to 1 overall, the troops under Henry V comprised 1500 men at arms and perhaps 7000 longbowmen. Anxious to avenge earlier defeats the mounted French nobility, said to number around 5000, charged across a muddy field towards the waiting archers. Under a hail of arrows and bogged down the French simply piled up in front of Henry's lines. The outcome was disastrous for the French who lost, some say, 10 000 men in total. For the English and Welsh archers it was a triumph – made all the more glorious through the long lens of history, not least by Shakespeare in his St Crispin's day speech put into the mouth of the young king.

This one-off disaster by no means heralded the end of the cavalry as a fighting force – indeed Agincourt was an aberration – and horse power continued to rule the battlefields of Europe for another four centuries. What faint lesson might be drawn by future military leaders was that given the right defensive weaponry (the longbow, light and manoeuvrable, was a major technological advance of its day) on a battlefield where the rapid movement of mobile forces was restricted, the recognised balance of power was in doubt. Coincidentally Agincourt, Azincort today, lies in the modern Département of Pas-de-Calais where much of the fighting on the Western Front took place, neighbouring the Somme.

'The Battle of Edgehill' by Thomas Stothard (1755–1834).

Also in October, but two centuries later, two English armies lined up against each other at the first significant battle of the English Civil War at Edgehill. The Royalist army under King Charles I and commanded by Prince Rupert numbered around 12 500 troops, the Parliamentary army slighter more numerous at 15 000. The two were evenly matched in mounted troops with around 2500 horse and 750 dragoons (musketeers mounted on horseback), but the Royalist cavalry were superior tactically and more experienced in mounted action. Oliver Cromwell (who arrived too late to take part in the battle although he witnessed its end), comparing the two forces had written disparagingly 'Your troopers are most of them old decayed servingmen and tapsters; and their troopers [the King's] are gentlemen's sons, younger sons and persons of quality.'

While the outcome of the 1642 battle itself was indecisive it is generally acknowledged that, had the Royalist cavalry not set off in random pursuit of a fleeing enemy and to plunder their baggage train, the King would have carried

the day. For Oliver Cromwell the battle was a spur to setting up and training a more professional fighting unit. Having a few months before Edgehill mustered a troop of horse, less than a year later he was commissioned as Colonel and expanded his troop into a full regiment in the newly formed Army of the Eastern Association. By 1644 this had grown into a double regiment comprising 14 troops of horse, and Cromwell had become Lieutenant General of the Horse in the Parliamentary Army. That year the regiment, known as Ironsides after their commander, played a decisive role in the Battle of Marston Moor. Increasingly highly trained and disciplined, and fortified by their belief that glory in battle was the work of God, Cromwell's cavalry became the core of the New Model Army, its successs culminating in the Battle of Naseby in 1645 where the main Royalist army was destroyed.

Thus the power of the horse brought about the downfall of the English king, and while Cromwell's skill at organising armies did not extend to running a country, his role in the English Civil War reinforced the importance of trained and disciplined mounted troops even on a battlefield where the use of artillery had come into its own.

It was the Napoleonic Wars that ran from 1803 to 1815, and in particular The Battle of Waterloo that revealed the horse-versus-artillery war at its spectacular and horrific best. Wellington's cavalry numbered 14 000, a thousand fewer than Napoleon's mounted troops, and were considered superior in terms of the quality of the horses but, as with the Royalist horse in the Civil War, maintained a reputation for running away with themselves in pursuit of the enemy rather than pressing home an advantage in the field.

The famous Charge of the Royal Scots Greys at the Battle of Waterloo – an oil painting by Elizabeth Kitson.

Lionising victorious generals through artworks goes back to the earliest civilisations, with the representation and symbolism changing little over the centuries. Here Jacques Louis David (1748–1825) commemorates Napoleon's crossing of the Alps in a typically idealised portrait in 1800.

By this date the distinction between light and heavy cavalry was becoming blurred. The cavalry's main role on the battlefield was as a shock force, battering into the enemy's lines in carefully orchestrated and rehearsed formations, disrupting any forward movement on the part of the opposing troops and creating opportunities for their own infantry to exploit.

The footsoldiers' response to this was to form squares, an ancient tactic but perfected during the Napoleonic Wars by both sides. Anywhere between 500 and 1000 men would form a hollow square or rectangle with two or more ranks of riflemen facing towards the enemy. Famously the four-rank squares at Waterloo withstood eleven separate cavalry charges.

But battlefield artillery was coming into its own and doing great execution against both infantry and mounted troops. The sheer carnage resulting from grape shot, canister shot and exploding shells falling amid densely packed troops and animals can only be imagined. One observer on approaching Waterloo describes the distant sound of guns 'rolling like a sea in the distance', and on nearing the field of battle heard 'the horses scream at the smell of corruption'.

The effect of artillery on men and horses is also described by Alexander Cavalier Mercer who compiled a vivid journal of the campaign, including the events which overtook a battery of the Royal Horse Artillery during the Battle of Waterloo.

Horse against horse. The 7th Hussars charging the French cavalry at Waterloo. An oil painting by Henry Martens (1825–1865).

One shell I saw explode under the two finest wheel-horses in the troop – down they dropped. In some instances the horse of a gun or ammunition waggon remained and all their drivers were killed. Our gunners too – the few left fit for duty – were so exhausted that they were unable to run the guns up after firing, consequently every round they retreated nearer to the limbers... they soon came together in a confused heap, the trails crossing each other, and the whole dangerously near the limbers and ammunition waggons, some of which were totally unhorsed, and others in sad confusion from the loss of their drivers and horses, many of them lying dead in their harness attached to their carriages.

A French Cuirassier. An etching by Hippolyte Bellangé (1800-1866).

But in one case at least, a horse exacted its own revenge. The Baron de Marbot, a Lieutenant General in Napoleon's army describes in his memoirs a remarkably troublesome horse, Lisette, he took to war. Such was the animal's ferocity that it took five men to saddle her 'you could only bridle her by covering her eyes and fastening all four legs; but once you were on her back, you found her an incomparable mount.'

Lisette had already bitten several people when she was cured of the habit by a horseman the Baron had engaged in his service who 'armed himself with a good hot roast leg of Mutton. When the animal flew at him to bite him he held out the mutton; she seized it in her teeth... gave a scream and was perfectly submissive. Lisette became as docile as a dog.'

Later, amid the battle of Eylau in East Prussia, the Baron mounted on Lisette was attacked by a Russian grenadier who, in attempting to bayonet the Baron, drove his weapon into the horse's flank.

Her ferocious instincts being restored by the pain, she sprang at the Russian, and at one mouthful tore off his nose, lips and eyebrows, and all the skin of his face, making him a living death's head, dripping with blood. Then hurling herself with fury among the combatants, an officer who had made many attempts to strike me tried to hold her by the bridle; she seized him by his belly and carrying him off with ease, she bore him out of the crush to the foot of a hillock, where, having torn out his entrails and mashed his body under her feet, she left him dying on the snow.

And after the battle, what became of the wounded horses? Captain Rees Howell Gronow, an Old Etonian who fought at Waterloo, leaves this account.

After the battle of Waterloo, all the wounded horses of the Household Brigade of cavalry were sold by auction. Sir Astley Cooper attended the sale, and bought twelve, which he considered so severely hurt as to require the greatest care and attention in order to effect a cure. Having had them conveyed, under the care of six grooms, to his park in the country, the great surgeon followed, and with the assistance of his servants, commenced extracting bullets and grape-shot from the bodies and limbs of the suffering animals. In a very short time after the operations had been performed, Sir Astley let them loose in the park; and one morning, to his great delight, he saw the noble animals form in line, charge and then retreat, and afterwards gallop about, appearing greatly contented with the lot that had befallen them. These manoeuvres were repeated generally every morning, to his great satisfaction and amusement.

Throughout the Victorian period painters and sculptors continued to capture their subjects' and the public's mood for heroic figures presented in a classical mode. Lifesize bronzes, often paid for through public subscription, adorned municipal parks the length and breadth of the country.

This magnificent bronze statue of The Duke of Wellington was sculpted by Sir John Steel (1804–1891) and erected outside Register House, Edinburgh in 1852, amid great celebration.

And as in previous epochs, the rewards for the victor came not only in sharing in the spoils of war but in adulation from his countrymen. For Wellington, the Iron Duke, it meant an elevation almost to godlike status, and after Waterloo the public clamoured to acclaim him, notably at Wellington in Somerset, the town from which the Duke took his name. Here they erected a 53-metre-high obelisk as monument in his honour – one among a number of such edifices. Any number of statues of the Duke on horseback were erected including in London, Glasgow, Edinburgh, and at his home Apsley House. The statue now at Aldershot, originally sited at Hyde Park Corner, was the largest equestrian statue in Britain when it was completed in 1846.

The writer John Steinbeck noted: 'A man on a horse is spiritually as well as physically bigger than a man on foot', a fact that made the horse invaluable on the field of battle and inestimable as a sculptural symbol of power.

Britain's final war of the Victorian era was fought on the South African veldt against the Boers, an enemy who fully exploited the mobility of light cavalry against larger but more static British forces. Born horsemen, and excellent marksmen, the Boers constantly harassed the British infantry, their commanders adopting guerilla tactics, striking hard and fast and vanishing before reinforcements could arrive.

The gruelling nature of the war, fought in a barren environment and in an inhospitable climate took a terrible toll on the fighting men, thousands dying from disease. In all 75 000 lost their lives. But the war also presaged the catastrophic death toll of horses in the First World War – a number unprecedented up to that time. British mounts suffered particularly badly, not least from the privations of long sea voyages with little respite before being thrust into action. A general shortage of animals resulted in them being overladen which, combined with relentless marches and inadequate feed, resulted in a huge wastage. The average lifespan of a horse under British command was just six weeks.

During the epic sieges of Kimberley and Ladysmith, horses were a principal source of food for those besieged. This included a Bovril-like paste derived from boiling down horsemeat to be drunk as an equine equivalent of beef tea. In hastening to the relief of Ladysmith Sir John French's cavalry rode 500 horses to their death in a single day. Of little comfort to the 300 000 mules and horses which died in the South African War, were that lessons were learned that mitigated the suffering of horses during the First World War, including better care of animals in transit at sea.

Another casualty of the Boer War was General Sir Henry Redvers Buller, a soldier who had made a name for himself in the Zulu War in 1879, being awarded the VC for bravery under fire. Returning to South Africa twenty years later as commander of the

A horse is lifted from the deck of a British freighter landing at Port Elizabeth en route to the war against the Boers. Many animals did not survive the long sea journey and their life expectancy in South Africa was just six weeks.

The bronze Horse Memorial standing at Port Elizabeth commemorates the 300 000 animals killed in the Second Boer War.

THE WAR HORSES

General Buller's statue created by sculptor
Adrian Jones and erected in 1905.

REDVERS BULLER
V.C. C.C.B. C.C.M.C.
OF DOWNES

Natal field force his generalship left a good deal to be desired and, following a number of defeats, his troops gave him the nickname 'Reverse Buller'. He later redeemed his earlier setbacks by significant victories over the Boers and returned to England a hero. But the war was not going well and a scapegoat was called for. Buller was sacked. In his native Devon, however, the general remained a notable worthy and in 1905 subscribers raised money for a bronze statue to be erected in Exeter not far from his home in Crediton: a fallen hero elevated on a bronze charger.

While the gaining of public approval through military prowess (and consequently being celebrated through art) was a male preserve, royalty had its own privileges in this respect. Few, if any, reigning British monarchs have failed to have their personage immortalised – and elevated – through equine portraiture or sculpture. The portrait 'Queen Victoria on Horseback' by Sir Edwin Landseer must rank among the most fanciful of all royal portraits set as it is an antick medieval landscape, a painting in which the inclusion of the horse swerves away from the traditional portrayal of power and majesty towards a romanticised, even fey, depiction of the mounted monarch. The fact that the horse, Leopold, was in life the Queen's favourite does little to redeem the sentimentality of the picture.

Victoria's successor, Edward VII who reigned from 1901 to 1910, and his son George V, who was to reign throughout the years of the First World War, reverted more to the typical equine statuary of their forebears, and a number of notable examples exist. But theirs were to be among the last of their kind where man and horse share equally in a potent representation of indomitable sovereignty. The appetite for such symbolism was largely assuaged by the slaughter that began in 1914, ending forever the unquestioned notion of nobility in war; although the concept was by no means eradicated, as in the illustration 'Victory!', published in 1918.

Off To Fight the Foe

Goodbye Dolly I must leave you, though it breaks my heart to go.
Something tells me I am needed at the front to fight the foe.
See, the soldier boys are marching and I can no longer stay.
Hark, I hear the bugle calling, Goodbye Dolly Gray.

                                                    Popular song

There never was a such a defined moment, but in popular imagination the First World War created a breakwater diverting the flow of history, after which it was possible to discern a country once full of pride, self-belief and at peace with itself, thereafter a nation no longer sustained by its traditions.

The war in western Europe (with which this book is largely concerned) began in August 1914. The German army attacked through neutral Belgium, its right flank converging on Paris with the main body intent upon encircling the French army which had massed on the German border. By 12 September the French, now joined by the British, halted the enemy's advance at the First Battle of the Marne. This signalled the end of mobile warfare on the Western Front with trenches eventually becoming the front line of both armies. Barbed wire, machine guns, artillery and poison gas checked the ebb and flow of battle along a 400 mile line that meandered from the French coast to the Swiss border.

In Britain men were seized by an almost hysterical desire to 'go out and face the Hun' – with the flames of popular feeling being fanned by carefully orchestrated prop-

Propaganda ensured few could resist the call to volunteer. By January 1915 over a million men had joined up, but a year later, with numbers waning, the British government was obliged to introduce conscription.

Sporting summer boaters, city clerks escorted by Territorials join the tens of thousands who volunteered in August and September 1914 for what became known as Kitchener's army.

aganda. But while Kitchener, the Secretary of State for War, was able to raise a vast volunteer army of men, with 750 000 joining up by September 1914, the acute shortage of horses was a problem yet to be solved. For decades prior to the First World War horses had been exported to the Continent to serve in such conflicts as the Franco-Prussian War; the Government Committee set up in 1873 to look into the problem of shortage should another war occur came up with few answers. In the event of war it had been estimated that the army would have immediate need of 25 000 additional animals sufficient for the first six months of war, a target well beyond anything that could be provided by the home market. With few horses being available from Europe, and the costs of purchasing them growing, the Committee looked farther afield, their eye eventually falling on Canada. As one witness called before the Committee stated: 'I think it would be a very good thing to import Canadian horses in an emergency. They are as good troopers as I ever saw.'

But the reality was rather different, despite the enthusiasm of Canadian farmers to fill this lucrative need. The army would pay $150 for a cavalry horse and $175 for an animal capable of hauling artillery, no small sum when the average annual wage for a manual worker was $375. A Colonel Ravenhill travelled throughout Canada in 1887 at the behest of the Committee to look at the possibility of supply through the Queen's Dominion. He was disappointed. Of the 75 000 horses he was shown, only a thousand were worthy of serious examination of which only 80 were purchased.

Meanwhile the Remount Department, set up in 1887, continued to operate it registration scheme through which 'owners of horses could register a proportion of their horses under an agreement to produce a number of horses at a fixed price in the event of their being required'. By 1899 14 000 horses were registered, but this was only 56 per cent of the number identified as being needed. Despite continued warnings the government refused to act, and when the Boer War broke out that year the situation regarding the supply of horses could have been disastrous.

Under the Army Act of 1881 the military were entitled to seize horses and carriages for use in an emergency under strict terms laid down in the Act. This required the authorities to keep and maintain 'a list of persons liable to furnish carriages and animals'. In March 1888 questions were raised in the House regarding the seizure of a number of horses and carriages in Donegal and in particular 'of one Anthony Donnell, of Maghera, [who] had his horse, cart, and load of flax seized and thrown into the yard of Miss Hegarty's hotel, the District Inspector refusing to allow the owner to take it to the market place, only 50 yards distant.' In reply the Secretary of State, Edward Stanhope, made clear the provisions of the Act had been complied with:

A large number of civilians worked for the Remount Department, including many women who helped break in and train horses. Indeed it is said that women formed the cornerstone of this unit during the war.

Horses and carts were impressed for the conveyance of baggage to Dunfanaghy in January last. Several of the drivers absconded en route, and their carts and horses were driven to Dunfanaghy by soldiers. As soon as the officer commanding found that the carts were no longer required he sent word to the owners that they could take them away; and that if they failed to do so the animals would stand at livery at the owners' risk and expense. A compensation was paid to those drivers who accompanied their carts. I am advised that the course taken by Colonel Kinloch would be considered a reasonable discharge by a County Court Judge acting under section 115 (4) of the Army Act. Anthony Donnell was, on the 2nd of February last, paid 11s., being at the rate of ½d. per cwt. per mile, going and returning. As the driver abandoned the cart at Letterkenny no compensation for detention was paid to him.

The public mistrust of enforced impressment was not confined to troublesome Ireland, and while the Act remained in force throughout the First World War (and was not finally repealed until 2006), the authorities began to recognise the urgent need to find other ways to fulfil the requirement for horses within army service.

In part technology came to the aid of the War Department. In many of Britain's cities tram lines were undergoing electrification, with horse-drawn trams being phased out, thus throwing on to the market hundreds of horses. A tram horse, once worth around £55, could now be purchased for as little as £43. This fortunate circumstance went some way towards mitigating the shortage of horses in South Africa in what was a mobile campaign largely reliant upon a constant supply of these animals.

The village blacksmith at Codford in Wiltshire finds himself busy shoeing horses for troops based at the nearby camp before they leave for the Front. The flood of recruits from the land left farmers short of labourers, their leaving not always due to a sense of patriotic spirit – as one worker recalled: 'When the farmer stopped my pay because it was raining and we couldn't thrash, I said to my seventeen-year-old mate. 'Bugger him, we'll go and join the army.'

A horse tram of the South Shields Tramways and Carriage Company which ran its trams with horses from around 1885 to 1906. The general introduction of electric trams from around 1900 onwards saw thousands of horses being thrown on to the market.

An electric tram in the south London suburb of Addiscombe c.1915. In London the first electric tram appeared in 1901, and by 1915 the last horse tram had been withdrawn. This rapid change from horse power to electrification rapidly depressed the livestock prices fetched by former carriage horses.

The war against the Boers, which continued until 1902, was a wake up call to the military who realised they had wildly underestimated the number of animals that would be required in a future conflict, not least due to wastage through death, injury and disease, a figure of 67 per cent in South Africa. In the ensuing decade further efforts were made to remedy the shortfall in horse power in the event of war but by 1914 that situation was by no means resolved.

On the outbreak of war in 1914 the provision of horses to the army fell entirely upon the shoulders of the Remounts Service from which the British Army drew all its horses and mules. At this time the Remounts Service was a small organisation comprising four squadrons within the Army Service Corps which was responsible for all transport within the army. Each squadron employed around 200 servicemen who took charge of and trained 500 horses. When the British Expeditionary Force embarked for France they took with them a Base Remount Depot with 2600 animals and two Advance Remount Depots with 300.

The Boer War had also provided important lessons regarding the mass transport of horses to the battlefield. Much of the wastage in animals occurred as a result of ignorance and poor facilities both on vessels and on the dockside. Anyone who has transported a horse will appreciate they are acutely sensitive to strange environments, refusing to move past an obstacle with which they are unfamiliar. Imagine then the journey undertaken by not one but by hundreds of horses (strangers to each other as well as to the noise the sights and the smells they were subjected to), from the depots by train to the dockside, then lifted aboard a ship where they might spend several weeks at sea, with the reverse process on arriving at their destination.

Shocked by his experiences during the Boer War, Captain M. Horace Hayes published in 1902 his instructive book *Horses on Board Ship: A Guide to Their Management*. He outlines his reasons for producing the book:

> *Fortunately, at the beginning of this year, I obtained veterinary charge of 498 remounts proceeding from England to South Africa, on board the hired cattle steamer* Kelvingrove *on which there were thirty-three nondescript men and boys to look after the animals; and after a most instructive passage I returned to England. Wishing to see how things were managed on board ship with troops, I [was sent] in veterinary charge of 248 remounts going to South Africa on H.M.T.* Idaho, *which also carried a large number of infantry and 110 men of the 10th Hussars. I therefore obtained an insight into both the civil and military methods of horse management at sea.*

The book provides a fascinating insight into the conditions horses would be subjected to, even on the comparatively short Channel crossings to the Western Front; although of course long-distance journeys were necessary for those animals being transported to and from more distant theatres of war between 1914–1918.

> *Under favourable arrangements and in small numbers, horses bear a sea voyage almost as well as a sojourn in a loose box for a similar period; but their percentage of mortality is generally high when the shipment is large. In this respect, their power of resistance is much less than that of mules; apparently because they are as a rule bigger; the weight of their bodies, as compared to the strength of their legs and feet, is heavier; and they are not so hardy.*

A photograph from Horses on Board Ship *showing an arrangement for stalls on the upper decks and captioned 'Horses in double stalls on a spar deck which is covered by a shade deck.'*

The author discuss the feeding of horses while in transit – 'although a horse in strong work can remain healthy while consuming a large daily ration of corn, he will be unable to do so, when kept in idleness, as he would be on board ship' – and various matters relating to their wellbeing on board – 'No provisions for allowing horses to lie

'Main deck of horse-carrying three-decker, showing stall at starboard side and midship stalls'. From Horses on Board Ship.

'On board stalls with single breast boards. Here there is a spare stall which is provided with a scupper between the two horses. At the top of this spare stall there is an india rubber water pipe which is folded up and out of the way'. From Horses on Board Ship.

Transporting horses by sea could be a costly business both in monetary terms and in lives lost. It is estimated that on the Atlantic crossing alone during the First World War over 6500 horses and mules were lost due to attack by submarines.

down or for giving them exercise need be made, if the length of the voyage does not exceed fourteen days.' On the question of mortality while at sea, he records that of the 49 000 horses shipped from Great Britain to South Africa 3000 died in transit, i.e. around 6 per cent. Some of this high mortality rate was due to incompetence:

For instance, when the SS Cervona, *on one of her horse-carrying voyages to South Africa, arrived one day in Algoa Bay, the inspecting veterinary surgeon who came on board was informed by the remount officer in charge that in consequence of an outbreak of glanders, 254 horses had been shot, and that he would have destroyed the remainder, had not the inclemency of the weather prevented him from throwing more carcasses overboard. A strict veterinary examination was thereupon held on the survivors, with the result that not the slightest indication of glanders was found among any of them. And thus, over £10,000 of public money was needlessly expended to feed Atlantic fishes.*

SUGGESTED DAILY RATION FOR HORSES ON BOARD SHIP

Bran, 6 lbs.
Hay, 17 lbs.
or
Oats, 3 lbs).
Bran, 3 lbs.
Hay, 17 lbs.
And, say, 5 lbs. of carrots in either case.

THE GOVERNMENT DAILY FORAGE SCALE FOR REMOUNTS AT SEA

Oats, 4 lbs.
Bran, 6 lbs.
Hay, 12 lbs.

Also, 4 cwt. nitre, 5 cwt. rock salt, plus 100 gallons vinegar, and 2 tons linseed are allowed for each shipment.

From *Horses on Board Ship* 1902.

But what is clear from this book and similar accounts and observations is the general concern, beyond any financial reasons, for the care and wellbeing of horses leading up to and during the First World War. Ignorance rather than cruelty brought about ill-treatment.

Hence, before horse attendants commence their duties on board ship, they should be seriously cautioned never to touch or threaten a horse's muzzle; and that when they are obliged to come up to an animal which is at all nervous or inclined to snap, they should hold up their hand at about the height of the upper part of his head, with the open palm turned towards him, and should gently pat his neck or rub his forehead with it while speaking to him in soothing tones. Everyone who has anything to do with horses should bear in mind that the human voice is one of the best and most powerful means for quietening and controlling horses. Both with troops and with 'cattle men' I have had very disheartening experience of the brutal manner in which they often treat horses at sea; their fault in this respect being probably due much more to ignorance and timidity than to deliberate cruelty.

General Seely, formerly Secretary of State for War, active in preparing the army for war with Germany, and who fought on the Western Front throughout, confirms the compassion generally shown for horses by the troops.

But I would like to record that one of the finest things about that indomitable creature, the English soldier of the front line, was his invariable kindness and, indeed, his gentleness at all times towards horses. I hardly ever saw a man strike a horse in anger during all the four years of war, and again and again I have seen a man risk his life and, indeed, lose it, for the sake of his horse.

FORWARD!

Forward to Victory
ENLIST NOW

But it was the shortfall in the number of horses required by the army that remained the overriding concern in August 1914. With only 25 000 in hand it was recognised that at least five times this number would have to be found immediately, the majority of these being acquired through impressment, purchase under the registration scheme and on the open market at home. Under the initial enthusiasm for war, no small number of animals were freely given for war service by individuals and companies anxious to 'do their duty', encouraged by the optimism that the war would be 'over by Christmas'. One such was a livery company owned by the Turner family of Kent who gave up all their animals for the cause never to see them again, with their thriving business simply disappearing.

The army later gave up on impressment and relied upon the general market, acquiring 469 000 animals from within Britain and the remainder imported from the USA, Canada, New Zealand, Australia, India, Portugal and Spain. It is estimated that over-

Battalion of the 2nd Lincolns at a camp in 1911. Note the number of horses required for what was an infantry battalion.

all the war consumed 8 million horses – a million on the Western Front by the Allies alone. A further 213 000 mules were in army service by the war's end.

In 1914 the British Army had an inventory of eighty motor vehicles only. Most of the transportation of equipment, guns, munitions and fuel had therefore to be undertaken by horse power. This was even more true of the German Army in which, on the eve of war, the ratio of horses to men had risen from one to four to one horse for every three men. In Britain the logistical hurdles that had to be overcome in August 1914 were daunting, but with the help of retired army officers who had stood by ready to help with the task of horse mobilization, in less than two weeks 165 000 horses had been 'recruited'. During the course of the war over 620 000 animals were landed at British ports, almost all of these from Canada and the USA. Between 1914 and 1920 the Remount Department spent £67.5 million on the purchase, training and delivery to the front of horses and mules.

And so the journey on the way to war had begun. In August 1914 that portion of the army earmarked for immediate service in France was the British Expeditionary Force of 125 000 men, comprising six divisions, supported by a further half million men including the Army Reserve and the Territorials. At that time a division was made up of approximately 18 000 men and 5500 horses. This included three infantry brigades, each of four battalions, three artillery brigades and one field howitzer brigade each with three batteries of 6 guns, and a heavy battery, all with their ammunition

Not much escaped the eye of the impressment officers. The fully loaded pony, formerly used to pull the baker's cart in Barnstaple, Devon, was requisitioned for use by the Army Service Corps in 1914. But it was not only horses that were 'borrowed' for the war effort, this RAC poster is dated August 1914, the first month of the war.

North Devon Yeomanry ride through Barnstaple in North Devon on being mobilized in August 1914.

columns. Two field companies of Royal Engineers, a cavalry squadron, signal companies, field ambulance and stretchers bearers, plus the Army Service Corps, made up the remainder of this complex element of men, horses and machinery.

Each division was accompanied by its supply train comprising around 450 men, 375 horses and mules, and 200 wagons. They serviced the needs of the division and, once in France, received their supplies via the Channel ports at railheads some miles behind the front lines. In later years light railways were built to bring supplies even closer to the front. From there it was up to horse power to resupply the troops, and on a landscape so often badly cratered by shellfire, horses and mules were the only means of transport – and where even they could not venture, manpower was the only alternative. To get to France men and horses would often entrain together for transit to one of the Channel ports. Once on the Continent a further train journey took them towards the front.

A recruiting poster exhorting 'men accustomed to horses' to sign up for the duration of the war to serve in the ASC.

Cavalry regiments comprised 549 men of whom 26 were officers. In 1914 a regiment included the regimental HQ, three squadrons and a machine gun section. Each squadron was made up of 227 men commanded by a Major. In total the regiment had a complement of 528 horses, with 48 in reserve, and 74 draught horses with 6 pack horses. Britain had increased its cavalry reserves following its experiences in the Boer War and indeed the first British shot fired in France was by cavalryman Edward Thomas of the Irish Dragoon Guards.

It was traditional that cavalry officers could choose their mounts or could provide their own chargers should they so wish, although strictly at their own expense, and in 1877 this arrangement had been the cause for a question to be raised in the House, as recorded in *Hansard*:

THE WAR HORSES

A horse show behind the lines c.1915. The photograph captures a lancer sergeant successfully 'tent pegging'. Galloping a full speed and lifting a tent peg from the ground with a spear or lance is an ancient sporting skill, success in which was held in high esteem among cavalry regiments.

Mr O'Bierne asked the Secretary of State for War, if he would consider the advisability of placing officers of Cavalry on the same conditions as officers of the Field Artillery for selecting chargers from the remounts, having regard to the fact that owing to the heavy expenditure imposed upon officers of Cavalry in purchasing chargers, sufficient candidates cannot be induced to enter this branch of the service.

Mr Gathorne Hardy replied: Officers of Field Artillery receive only dismounted pay and are mounted on troop horses, which do not become their own property. Officers of Cavalry and Horse Artillery, who receive a higher rate of pay to cover expenses of their chargers, have certain privileges given them as to selecting horses from the ranks at moderate prices. If the Cavalry officers are to be placed on the same footing as the Field Artillery, as the hon. Member suggests, they would have – first, to be reduced to Infantry rates of pay, and, secondly, they would have to ride troop horses not their own property. This would certainly, I think, be unpopular. I have only to add that there are no vacancies in Cavalry regiments except those kept open for sub-lieutenants still under garrison instruction.

That these privileges existed for cavalry officers undoubtedly helped to maintain their elite status – if you could not afford to keep your own horse you were unlikely to join a cavalry regiment. But there is no question that good quality horses were much admired, with individual animals raising the *esprit de corps* of a squadron or regiment. This was certainly true of General Seely's famed charger Warrior who, whenever they appeared together on the battlefield in front of the Canadian Cavalry Brigade, which Seely commanded, would be greeted with cheers and cries of 'Here comes old Warrior!' And it was not only the men who this magnificent animal inspired, as the General records.

We practised all kinds of manoeuvres, the idea being that the infantry were to break the German front line, and that the cavalry were then to sweep through the gap and take the enemy in the rear. We all played up to the part and did our utmost to get our horses as fit as possible, and well accustomed to machine-gun and rifle fire. Here Warrior's absolutely fearless nature was a great advantage. He set an example to all the other horses.

Keeping horses of quality in good condition near the front lines provided opportunities for sport between various units. In *Goodbye*

Judging the officers' chargers at a horse show behind the lines c.1915.

Competitors in the section-jumping at a horse show behind the lines c.1915.

A group of civilians in Wilton, Wiltshire stand in front of three makeshift army transports painted hastily with WD (War Department) insignia. Before war production of purpose-built mechanised transport got underway the army used every kind of civilian transport available, including London buses.

to All That Robert Graves, serving with the Royal Welch Fusiliers in France, is told by a fellow officer. 'We've even got a polo ground here. There was a polo match between the First and Second Battalions the other day. The First had all their decent ponies pinched last October when they were massacred at Ypres. So the Second won easily.' Graves has a jaundiced view of such activities: 'But this is all childish. Is there a war on here or isn't there?' to which came the superbly laconic response 'The Royal Welch don't recognize it socially.'

General Seely exhibits more enthusiasm for these impromptu competitive events, recognising the importance of them in keeping the horses fit and the men in a competitive frame of mind: 'At intervals in the lull of battle we would have sports, including horse shows. Warrior and I used to put up some sort of show when we happened to be out of line.'

But it was the more mundane tasks of fetching and carrying in which the majority of horses were engaged; hauling guns and ammunition, pulling wagons and ambulances, and carrying general supplies. Specialist tasks such as carrying cable drums for the Royal Corp of Signals and acting as mounts for dispatch riders also fell to the horses. The lack of mechanised vehicles for use by the army in 1914 has already been touched upon and those lorries and tractors that could be found, often of dubious origin and reliability, were sometimes secured by devious means, as Robert Graves records somewhat enigmatically.

Apart from a few traction engines for pulling heavy siege guns, the BEF was completely unmechanised until, at the last moment, a couple of Royal Engineers officers were sent to commandeer a few score brewery lorries. No provision, of course, had been made for a supply of magnetos, and the disgraceful story of how the war office obtained them by secret trading with the Bosch Company of Stuttgart has never yet, I believe, been told.

A Field Ambulance (FA) unit was another specialist part of a division and one that only existed in wartime, being formed as part of the Royal Army Medical Corps on the outbreak of war. Each division held three FA units, one to each brigade, comprising nine Medical Officers, a quartermaster and about 40 Army Service Corps drivers. In all it included about 78 horses of the heavy draught and light draught type. In a fascinating diary kept by Travis Hampton MC he records the amount of kit each of the officers' horses were expected to carry.

The officers' valises, limited to 35 pounds in weight, are carried in front on our saddles, the iron ration, socks, washing kit and anything that could be crammed in, the great coat being rolled and strapped behind the cantle of the saddle. On yourself, a regular Christmas Tree, as it came to be known. Sam Browne belt, haversack, water bottle, field glasses, map case, whistle, pocket instrument case, revolver and ammo pouch. On the horse: a saddle, with the things already mentioned, also a head rope, a heel rope (on some), a nose bag, a body brush and rubber, a canvas bucket, two spare horse shoes in case, a sword, a picketing peg, and a saddle blanket. The total weight carried by the horse is about seventeen and a half stone on average, depending of course quite a bit on the weight of the rider. I believe a cavalry horse has to carry even more.

A Field Ambulance wagon appears at a horse show put on behind the lines. The two greys have been groomed for the parade and the wagon is highly polished, a scene that is a far cry from the reality of ambulances working on the front line as the photograph on the following pages shows.

"When we reached the ruins of the village it was a dreadful sight: mutilated bodies of men and horses and mules everywhere among which we had to shelter while waiting a chance to run the gaunlet around a spot known to us as Suicide Corner."

Joseph Murray

On embarking for France in August 1914 Captain Hampton describes some of the difficulties encountered when loading horses on to trains.

There was a little trouble with some of the horses. Many of them are huge beasts, and could hardly hold their heads up in the cattle trucks. Entraining instructions stated – 'if there is any trouble in getting a horse in, two drivers should lock arms above his hocks and hustle him in'. Our ASC drivers are all very small, though tough, and it struck us as rather amusing to see two small men trying to hustle an enormous draught horse that had other ideas on the subject. But by getting a willing one in first, there was not too much difficulty.

Motor ambulances eventually replaced many horse-drawn units in France. This is one of a remarkable series of autochromes (an early colour process), taken on the Western Front.

Hampton's FA unit was completely horse-drawn 'there are no motor vehicles. This applied to the whole of the original British Expeditionary Force, except for a few staff cars and motor cyclists, and the motor lorry supply columns.' Although lorries would eventually replace the horse-drawn ambulances, in some instances the latter were more effective in reaching parts of the battlefield that were so badly shell-torn that motor vehicles were of no use.

Previous page: The flying of a red cross flag has not saved this German field ambulance or its horses from destruction. The scene appears to be at a forward dressing station or Regimental Aid Post just behind the German lines. Smoke still rises from the buildings obliterated by shellfire as men attempt to extricate a dead or dying horse from its harness. Several other horses lie dead.

In a scattered action, naturally the wounded will be all over the place, many will never get to the Regimental Aid Post, and have to be searched for and collected together for dressing or evacuation. The next step in the evacuation is the carriage of the wounded from the RAP or round about to the FA Advanced Dressing Station (ADS). The position of this is of course extremely variable, depending on the situation, but if possible it is a place on a road where our horse buses can be got to, and where the wounded can be attended to, that is, those who need further attention before their next move.

Our real difficulty at first was to get the wounded back to a place where they could be properly attended to. The greatest want I think was motor ambulances, of which we had none in the BEF at first. Later we got 8 in place of 7 of our horse buses, keeping 3 horse buses as they could get to places where no motors could, especially such places as the Somme area in the Winter. Then it took a team of six horses instead of two for the job.

On originally arriving at the front, Hampton described the horses attached to his unit through the Army Service Corp.

After a few days the horses arrived with their ASC personnel. I chose my rider, a well made nice looking nag of about 15.2, strong, and in good condition. After this I had a ride every afternoon with the CO to Long Valley, or somewhere to call on people he knew round about. My nag very fresh, on the jog all the time, very difficult to make him walk. I hope it will wear off later; he is very fast, but can't jump. Except for the CO, the other officers seem rather to dislike the sight of their horses, and several of them I think have never been on a horse before.

The riders on the whole seem to be rather on the small side, in any case, the average MO doesn't want, and certainly won't get, a cavalry officer's charger. But we have some very fine requisitioned hunters getting to some of the FAs. The draught horses, also the riders, are all civilians, and quite new to Army life. The heavies are a magnificent lot; they are the pick of the brewer's drays and such like horse drawn civilian transport. The light draught also appear to be first rate. I believe the Government has a scheme to subsidise owners in exchange for the liability to requisition the horses when wanted.

On drawing the ambulances and other vehicles there was a lot of work to be done checking every item and all the stores and to get to know exactly where any particular thing should be and was carried. Quite a job was pairing the draught horses and fitting the harness, all of which was delivered in its parts with nothing put together, and when assembled, each bit had to be fitted to the individual horse.

Whether embarking by boat or by train the transport of horses could prove difficult and dangerous. This original autochrome is captioned 'British Artillery Embarking for France'.

The mention of pairing the horses is worthy of note, for to those familiar with working horses this was of fundamental importance in their management in drawing a carriage or wagon where two horses work side by side. A good ploughman or wagoner taught his horses to pull equally (two horses pulling together can move several times more than their combined individual power), and also such tricky manoeuvres as how to turn into gateways with a wagon behind. Loaned horses, those requisitioned or obtained through the registration scheme came from all over Britain; it was unlikely that they had ever worked together before and therefore training was vital.

In the first months of the war Hampton paints a rather rosy picture of his life at the front. 'To me the 1914 war in its early days was all very exciting and intensely interesting. A horse damaged by shell fire or a civilian killed by enemy action were novelties, as for that matter a dead soldier or wounded also.' But as the months wore on the shortage of horse transport began to tell:

THE WAR HORSES

We had no motor ambulances for some time, and no motor ambulance convoys to collect from the HQ of the FA. Our horse buses were usually too fully occupied in the more forward area to take cases down the line. We had to rely at first on returning empty supply wagons to take the wounded that first stage from us.

It was the task of stretcher bearers to collect the wounded from the battlefield and trenches, getting them to the Regimental Aid Post which was sited as close as possible to the front line. Thereafter, sometimes via Collecting Posts, those in need of further treatment were carried by RAMC stretcher bearers to the Advanced Dressing Station controlled by the Field Ambulance and sited a few hundred yards back from the front. From there further treatment took place at Casualty Clearing Stations some miles behind the front line and eventually at a Base Hospitals. Horse-drawn ambulances or motor transport ferried between these various posts where the distance was too great for a stretcher party. Sometimes ration parties bringing rations up to the front by horse or mule would return with wounded men.

In difficult terrain is was necessary to use more horses than usual even when taking relatively light loads up to the front. Here a wagon slides off into an old trench system and gets bogged down.

The roads behind the front lines were often hardly better than the sea of liquid mud that comprised the fighting areas. Columns of troops, motor transport and

horse-drawn vehicles constantly plied backwards and forwards across packed-earth highways that in summer threw up clouds of choking dust and in winter became a morass. In *The Long Carry*, a book based on the diaries of stretcher bearer Frank Dunham, there is a graphic description of one such road.

The road was ankle deep in mud and slush, and in a very bad state owing to the continual shelling, and was crowded with all kinds of transport and troops – naturally the infantry came off worst as the horses splashed us all over with mud.

So deep was the winter mud that horses and men simply got stuck and sometimes died. Here a mule team lies helplessly, unable to move.

THE WAR HORSES

The Royal Army Medical Corps, as already referred to, also required horses for ambulances, taking wounded back from the lines to the Base Hospitals. Each army provided for its own wounded, and the type of vehicle varied widely, but as with other units the RAMC often found that horses could go where no lorry could – a vital factor in the rapid movement of serious cases. Time and again we are reminded in memoirs and diaries that the roads leading to and from the front sometimes presented such challenges that, even when not under shellfire, troops often arrived at their intended destination in a state of collapse, if they arrived at all. Hampton describes one such journey.

The road to the front. An officer's staff car sits at the end of a queue of transport stretching as far as the eye can see. A body of men march along the right-hand side passing a mule and an RAMC lorry. A pair of mules pulling a GS wagon heads a line of transport coming the other way.

We went on and on what seemed about 10 kilometres, and thought we must have lost our way. It was pitch dark and raining. Just then we came upon a reserve park of rations or ammunition. I don't know which, but it was miles of horse drawn GS wagons and an awful job getting by them in a narrow road with most of their drivers asleep. I think there must have been a good many splintered tail boards that night; the horses were just following the wagon in front, and if there was a check the pole of the following wagon was into the tailboard of the next before the horses could pull up.

An RAMC ambulance.

Field ambulances often contained racks on to which the wounded would be slid on their stretchers – a dozen or more at a time. The combined weight of these substantial vehicles, the crew and the wounded, would make any journey onerous for the horses – a task made more difficult on the dreadful road surfaces. Here a French ambulance brings in wounded to a Base Hospital. The original caption refers to the group of priests following – a sight which may or may not have been encouraging for the occupants.

This photograph provides a graphic image of conditions near the front lines, with ice edging pools of slurry-like mud along a narrow track. A false step either way could mean horse and man having to be hauled out. The original caption describes the men as walking towards the front line in order to ferry back the wounded on the crude wooden sledges being pulled by the horses.

THE WAR HORSES

Other units directly reliant upon horses included the Army Service Corps (later the Royal Army Service Corps), specialist units and the various artillery regiments. The ASC was literally the workhorse of the army and of the 800 000 or so horses and mules that were employed on the Western Front, the majority were in their hands. When the war began the ASC operated under two directorates, Transport and Movement and Supplies and Quartering but this was soon drawn under a single Director of Supplies and Transport, with units variously responsible for horse-drawn transport, mechanised transport, stores and warehousing, quarters for men and horses, railways, catering and, of course, remounts.

The US Army had always made greater use of mules (a cross between a female horse and a donkey) than the British Army, as these animals, despite their belligerent reputation, had a propensity for hard work and resilience under extreme conditions. Throughout the war the ASC used horses to mules in a proportion of around 3 to 1. Horse types varied widely and the tasks these animals performed ranged from performing duties as unofficial unit mascots to hauling great guns across the battlefield, but in almost all their areas of activity they were subject to stress, disease and outright danger resulting in a 50 per cent mortality rate when at the front.

Known by the troops as Ally Sloper's Cavalry (after a rent-dodging character in a popular humorous comic strip) the ASC on the Western Front numbered around 200 000 men. Much deprecated by the fighting soldier, ASC troops received little by way of recognition during or immediately after the war when other arms were being commemorated with statues and monuments. Their reputation was further hindered by the fact that

Troops struggle with duck boards which they are loading on to a pack horse. The original caption reads 'Everything was in readiness for the wet weather. Thousands of duck boards were sent forward as our troops advanced so as to make the going as easy as possible.'

A youthful ASC driver controls a handsome pair of draught horses hauling a tree trunk on a timber wain. At the front timber was in great demand, not least in reinforcing dugouts in the trenches.

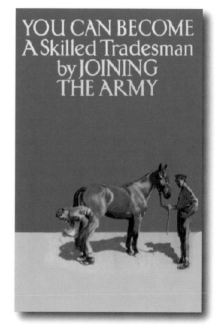

A similar pair of draught horses haul this wagon which carries a half section of corrugated sheeting, possibly for use in a dugout. The driver has found a novel way of protecting himself from the summer's sun.

This remarkable photograph show just a tiny part of the massive stores at the depot in Rouen in 1915. Every kind of supplies was routed here by cross Channel traffic via the River Seine. A motor lorry and two horse-drawn carts stand waiting, either having delivered material from the railhead or they are about to pick up rations for onward transit.

Back at home, the railways largely preserved their pre-war stock of horses as the army recognised the important role played by the railway transport system in getting material to the front.

"Loading the ship was a slow job. She was high above the quay, t tide being in. There were two electric cranes going. T vehicles were slung up by their hubs, and the horses with a sli under their bellies. The riders were slung up in a box. The heav looked rather funny high up in the air. They looked a bit scare which no doubt they were, and you had to stand clear when they landed, because as soon as their feet touched down nearly all of them tried to jump off the floor." Travis Hampton MC, 1914

Unloading stores at a railhead in France c.1916. The photograph illustrates perfectly the dilemma between the necessity for horse power balanced against the huge logistical cost of supplying fodder. Note the wagon in the foreground piled high with hay.

many Colonial and Empire troops were drafted into the ASC in order to release British troops into the front line forces to replace casualties, undermining the cohesion and *esprit de corps* enjoyed by regular forces. In reality the ASC suffered heavy casualties, with 2600 men being killed in action and with the award of two VCs for gallantry under fire.

While pack horses were ideal for moving relatively light loads rapidly over short distances, and mules were useful for this too, it was the ubiquitous four-wheeled General Service (GS) wagon that moved the bulk of material on the Western Front. Hauled usually by two, four, or six animals these wagons were manufactured in their thousands and operated throughout all theatres of war.

The ASC also provided horses for hauling large artillery pieces. Teams of up to twenty heavy horses could be employed to pull the largest guns into place although tractors

Above: *Men, material and horses being towed by barge along the River Seine towards the main Army Stores Depot at Rouen.*

Above right: *Attempting to rescue a pair of mules from deep mud. The original caption to this photograph states somewhat laconically 'Transport difficulties in the swamps of Flanders'.*

Below: *A heavy artillery train.*

Six-horse teams pulling GS wagons travel along dusty summer roads in France.

of various types eventually took over. On the road, guns of 4.7in calibre and above were hauled by four pairs of horses, the whole train moving at a steady plod, and once the guns were in place the horses were taken back to safety.

This was not the case with the various field artillery regiments incorporating the Royal Horse Artillery (attached to cavalry brigades) and the Royal Field Artillery (attached to division), whose horses were part of the battery and stayed with, or close to the guns, during engagements. The Honourable Artillery Company, the oldest surviving regiment in the British Army, was a Territorial Force, much smaller in size. Highly trained, fast and manoeuvrable, of all the forces employing horses in a combative role in the First World War, the artillery could be said to have been the least anachronistic, at least before the stagnancy of trench warfare set in. The RHA, employing 13 pounder guns, were considered more mobile than the RFA who were equipped with 18 pounders.

Responsibility for supplying ammunition fell to the Ammunition Column in the first two years of the war and each column included 18 limbered ammunition wagons, three 6-horse GS wagons, three 4-horse GS wagons, and seven 2-horse carts for rifle ammunition, along with farriers, shoeing smiths etc. Never far from the action, and recipients of many battle honours, these columns were subject to heavy casualties both in men and horses.

One of the most celebrated of these actions took place in early weeks of the war during the retreat from Mons on the morning of 24 August 1914. Having fought a successful rearguard action which saved the left wing of the allied armies from being cut off, Sir Horace Smith-Dorrien continued his orderly withdrawal in the face of increasingly stiff opposition. The artillery took particularly heavy casualties in horses and men, faced as they were with four times their own number of guns – mostly of higher calibre than their own. Individual batteries fought running engagements with the enemy, halting long enough to check advances then galloping off to new positions. But the shells from German howitzers had decimated many batteries, slaughtering horses and men alike.

As their superior numbers began to tell the enemy pressed forward on a general front opposed only by small groups of guns covering the allied withdrawal. One of these

Originally captioned 'feeding the guns during an advance', this war artist's impression of delivering ammunition under fire reflects the coolness required by the drivers who led teams of horses into the heat of battle. Horses wait patiently as men sweat to unload shells from a GS wagon while in the background an artillery shell explodes among the horses and men of another wagon.

was led by Captain Douglas Reynolds of the 37th Battery RFA who, seeing that all the horses attached to a number of guns had been killed, brought up two new teams in the hope of rescuing the guns. Driven by volunteers, and within a 100 yards of the enemy, the teams attempted to hitch up two guns to drag them away. Under a hail of fire one whole team was shot down, and the driver of the second was shot from his saddle. A contemporary report records what happened next:

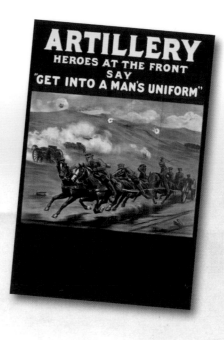

Captain Reynolds rode alongside the unguided pair of horses, and kept them in hand, with Driver Luke driving the leaders and Driver Drain the wheelers; the gun was brought safely out of action. Each of these three heroes was awarded the Victoria Cross, and one of them, Captain Reynolds, had the satisfaction of distinguishing himself again a fortnight later at the battle of the Marne, when, reconnoitring at close range, he located a battery which was holding up our advance and silenced it.

As the war progressed the opportunities for such individual acts of courage and derring-do grew fewer as the fluidity of the fighting in the first few months grew into a stalemate behind lines of trenches and miles of wire. General Haig's contention that the mobility of the cavalry would remain an essential adjunct to firepower fell at the first rattle of the machine guns emplaced defensively – turning the sweeping landscape of Flanders into killing fields.

'Men of the RFA cleaning their guns' a watercolour sketch by war artist Muirhead Bone (1876-1953).

Yet from 1915 onwards those men and horses responsible for moving, firing and supplying the guns faced even greater dangers from a largely faceless enemy now entrenched upon a static battlefield but enjoying, in the main, elevated positions from which it was possible to follow and plot any Allied movement. Artillery could be ranged on to specific targets using predetermined coordinates at a few minutes' notice, while indirect machine gun fire could be used to regularly rake positions where troop movements were known to take place, especially at night.

Such a place is described by Frank Dunham in *The Long Carry*.

A large sign proclaims the approach to Hell-fire Corner, one of the most notorious junctions on the Menin Road which ran from Ypres towards the front lines, and which was kept under constant surveillance by the Germans who shelled it at every opportunity. The canvas screens on the left were a poor attempt to hide movement from observers, and columns moving to and from the front were wise not to tarry here. It was one of several similar junctions on the Western Front, each luridly named – Shrapnel Corner was another – and often signposted as a warning to passing troops.

So far things had seemed strangely quiet, the only sound being that of our transport taking rations and ammunition up to the line dumps. We found ourselves on the open

'Royal Horse Artillery going into action at the gallop', reads the original caption to this photograph which shows a gun limber flying into the air as it passes over a low bank. These light guns and their limbers were, until the introduction of armoured cars and light tanks, the mobile arm of the artillery and used widely in the support of infantry. One infantryman described the scene on a busy road to the front lines: 'There is no end to the continual stream of every conceivable form of warfare passing through; artillery pieces of all shapes and sizes, horse drawn eighteen-pounders bouncing like shuttlecocks as they negotiate huge potholes.'

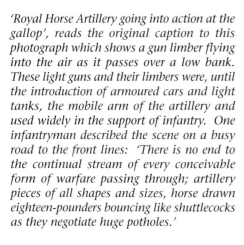

OFF TO FIGHT THE FOE

highway and Very lights could be seen bursting in the distance. The road was ankle deep in mud and slush, and in a very bad state owing to continual shelling, and was crowded with all kinds of transport, guns and troops. A little way up the road we were told this was the famous Shrapnel Corner, and soon passed places known as Transport Farm and Jackson's Dump. The latter place was as far as our transport came with our rations and carrying parties had to meet them nightly here and take the rations on foot to the line. This dump was well known to Fritz and, being on rising ground, he could drop machine gun bullets around the place nicely, and often inflicted casualties.

Artillerymen loading ammunition on to limbers before proceeding to the front. The horses attached to these batteries, pulling limbers and guns, were amongst the hardest-worked animals of the war.

"Ten Days before the end, the battery was in action before Le Quesnoy. The guns were in a little field, sloping down to a stream on the other side of which was a large mill. The only road to the front ran over the bridge past the mill. All day long columns of men, guns and transport passed over this bridge, and all day long the enemy shelled it with a high-velocity gun. In the afternoon when the gunners had ceased firing they lay back on the grass and speculated which of the endless teams of horses and mules, limbers and guns would get safely across the bridge. The sappers were working hard at repairs under this steady shell-fire. A gallant party of military police and others were clearing away the dead horses and men that littered the road both sides of the stream. A gun team would come trotting down the hill towards the bridge and a hundred yards from it, break into a gallop. 'Hooray! they are safely across. Here comes the next lot! Bang! That's got them. No, it hasn't–! as horses and men, less one driver, emerge from the smoke, and gallop up the road into safety on the other side."

Lt-Col. Lushington.

Wagons and limbers destroyed by shellfire, the wreckage and the bodies of horses pushed aside to make way for passing columns. This photograph was taken on the Italian Front.

Seen from the air, horse-drawn wagons taking ammunition to the guns in action generated an even greater sense of excitement, as Cecil Lewis describes.

I shall remember forever the Horse Artillery coming up into action behind Flers, on a road that was mostly shell holes, under a hail of shrapnel. A team of six roan chargers, sweeping up at full gallop, dumping ammunition by the guns and, with hardly a pause, galloping back again, the outriders crouching low over the necks of their plunging beasts with their flying manes and terrorstruck eyes! There isn't much picturesque or visibly heroic to be seen in this war when you are in the air – but that was!

Finally, among the troops reliant upon horses were the men of the Pioneer Corps and the Non Combatant Labour Corps. The Pioneer Corp units engaged in many light engineering duties, but were also called upon to fight. The NCLC men, often of reduced medical status, performed duties such as sanitary arrangements, road-building and other tasks, considered beneath that of regimental Pioneer Battalions. Nonetheless the role these men fulfilled, along with the animals in their care, was important to the overall success of prosecuting the war.

Members of the 4th Battalion Coldstreamers, a regimental Pioneer unit. Not only were these Pioneers fighting men (as opposed to the Non Combatant Labour Corps, which became the Pioneer Corps in the Second World War), it was also their role to provide labour. In this photograph the men appear to be quarrying stone for roadbuilding.

Into the Valley of Death

While the long-awaited breakthrough on the Western Front for the cavalry never came, there were several early actions in which cavalry forces engaged on horseback, often with each other, and usually as a result of small reconnaissance parties running into each other accidently. With bravura often getting the better of commonsense these skirmishes had little effect on the main conflict although the occasional victory by either side in the first months of the war furnished newspapers with stories of heroism and valour. For the readers at home this was still a war of chivalric romanticism – and a war that would certainly be 'over by Christmas'.

A fanciful depiction by a German artist of German troops repulsing the attack of British cavalry in the form of the 18th Hussars and 4th Dragoon Guards at Thulin, 1914. Much exaggerated – the actual event was relatively minor – the artist gave the German public what they wanted – heroism of the infantry in the face of massed cavalry attack.

Generally, however, the mounted forces of all armies were outdated both in the way they were equipped and in their thinking. Photographs taken in the early months of the war show mounted troops resplendent in impractical brass helmets and shining breastplates, parading much as they had in peacetime.

Dashing but outmoded, after 1914 cavalry units soon abandoned their horses for rifles and packs. Clockwise from top: French Cuirassiers leading a column of German prisoners, French Cuirassiers treating a wounded comrade, German Uhlans, Austro-Hungarian cavalry.

Field Marshal Sir John French, Commander of the BEF, recognised that cavalry would continue to perform an important role in reconnaissance duties, yet even in those early days it was aerial reports that were becoming the principal means by which information was gained concerning the enemy's movements. Writing of August 1914 French states 'This was our first practical experience in the use of aircraft for reconnaissance purposes . It cannot be said that in these early days of the fighting the cavalry entirely abandoned that role. On the contrary they furnished me with useful information.' French was not a great proponent of cavalry but he

recognised the conspicuous part they played in the first few weeks of the war. On one occasion he called into the HQ of the 169th Battery of the RFA whose guns had been at the centre of one of the great heroic cavalry actions fought in 1914. 'I visited in particular one Artillery Brigade, some of whose guns had been saved from capture on the previous day by the cavalry. The Brigade Commander broke down with emotion as he recounted to me the glorious bravery displayed by Francis Grenfell and the 9th Lancers'.

The action to which French refers occurred on 24 August 1914 at Audregnies, Belgium. Captain Grenfell rode with the regiment in a charge against a large body of unbroken German infantry. Casualties were very heavy and the captain was left as the senior officer. He was rallying part of the regiment behind a railway embankment when he was twice hit and severely wounded. In spite of his injuries, however, when asked for help in saving the guns by Major Ernest Wright Alexander of the 119th Battery, Royal Field Artillery, he and some volunteers, under a hail of bullets, helped to manhandle and push the guns out of range of enemy fire. Grenfell was awarded the VC.

But it was becoming clear to the military commanders that cavalry forces were most effective when fighting on foot alongside infantry units, exchanging lances and

Captain F.O. Grenfell VC from a stamp produced for The Lord Roberts Memorial Fund Album in 1915. The commentary provided with the stamp reads 'Captain F.O. Grenfell VC. One of the famous polo playing brothers – both killed in action. Won VC for great gallantry in action at Audregnies, Belgium, when with the 9th Lancers, charging against unbroken infantry. Later on the same day made heroic efforts to save the guns of the 119th Battery RFA, August 24 1914. Subsequently died from wounds. Previously served with great distinction in the South African War, 1901–2.'

General Sir Douglas Haig was dedicated to the cause of the cavalry. Even as late as 1927 he made the remark 'aeroplanes and tanks are only accessories to a man on a horse'. In December 1915, Haig replaced General Sir John French at which time French returned to England as Commander-in-Chief of the British Home Forces. According to General Seeley 'French was a very fine horseman, and loved and understood horses'.

77

THE WAR HORSES

swords for bayonets and rifles. But this had inherent problems as Sir John French explains in his memoir *1914*:

The Royal Scots Greys near Montreuil in 1918. By this time the elite cavalry units were as adept at fighting on foot alongside the infantry as they were on horseback. Note the more standard field uniform worn in contrast to the more flamboyant uniforms of the early war years, and also the rifles in the scabbards on their chargers.

For the information of non-military readers, it is necessary for me to explain that a cavalry division fighting on foot is at a great disadvantage as compared with an infantry division. When horses cannot be used in the fighting, they still have to be looked after, and this takes many men away from the fighting line. A cavalry division consists ordinarily of three brigades, but when employed in the trenches they get little more than half that number into the firing line. They have nothing like the same 'gun power' as an infantry division.

General Seely suggests that, even as late as 1915, such was the sensitivity of cavalry-men being asked to fight as infantry that it was treated as a matter for volunteering rather than as a direct order.

A colour autochrome photograph of the Royal Scots Greys from the First World War.

I was summoned to the War Office to see Lord Kitchener. He asked me: 'Will you take your command to Flanders at once, leaving all your horses behind? I make one condition if you say 'yes' as I know you will. The men themselves must volunteer to go without their horses. I know how much they love them, and I do not think it fair to order them against their will to go without them.'

I said 'You need not ask that question. Of course every man will volunteer.'

'That may be,' he replied, 'but I ask you to go back to them, and ask them to volunteer.'

In some respects General French might be said to be more forward-looking than the man who replaced him – General Sir Douglas Haig – a cavalry man through and through who remained optimistic to the end that cavalry would lead the final charge against the Germans once the breakthrough came, and almost a decade after the war's end still declared 'aeroplanes and tanks are only accessories to a man on a horse'. French held a more pragmatic view:

Of late years it has been our custom to train our cavalry to fight on foot, and in the present war we have reaped the fruit of this wise policy. But the instinct which must be inculcated in the horse soldier to regard his horse as his chief reliance, must always disqualify him to some extent for the role which our cavalry were called upon to fulfil throughout the momentous issues in the history of the (present) war.

A cavalry unit passing the ruins of Albert Cathedral in 1915. Increasingly effective weaponry combined with the attritional nature of trench warfare saw a dramatic decline in the strength of cavalry regiments in the British Army, from 7.2 per cent in 1914 to 1.01 per cent by the war's end.

Thus despite individual instances of heroics, and the insistence by Haig that sooner or later the cavalry would come into their own, the days of the cavalry fighting as an effective mounted force were almost numbered. Furthermore, as the war progressed the cavalry as a fighting arm was reduced so much physically in size that it ceased to be a decisive factor in military planning.

In a recently published thesis, 'British Cavalry on the Western Front 1916–1918' David Kenyon refutes the views 'ingrained in the psyche of Great War writers' that cavalry forces were outmoded, at the mercy of new technology – particularly machine guns – and that ultimately the costs of provisioning of horses would better be spent on weaponry rather than hay and oats. He cites instances in later battles where, had the cavalry been used in its traditional role rather than fighting on foot, a more positive outcome would have been achieved, and in battles where they *were* used, the cavalry were successful in exploiting gaps in the enemy's lines. The debate will continue but what is undoubtedly true is that the cost of keeping horses in the front line and the attrition rates caused in action and through sickness were leading to an inevitable preference for machines to achieve the necessary mobility required for victory. Across

Royal Scots Greys practising a charge in France during the First World War. The horses wear double bridles to give greater control. The men are in field uniform with standard issue steel helmets. Indeed, without their horses the men have every appearance of an infantry unit. It is said that they grey horses of the Royal Scots Greys caused some worries in 1914, when an order went out from Headquarters on 22 August 1914 that, 'since grey horses will make a conspicuous target, immediate steps will be taken to darken the colour of regimental chargers'. For a while there were unhappy experiments to dye the horses with a permanganate solution, measures soon abandoned.

Cavalry troopers sit at the edge of a shallow scrape and by the look of them appear either to be about to go into action, or having just returned from a fight. Despite the presence of the photographer they show little enthusiasm for playing up to the camera. The carrying of ammunition bandoliers around the necks of their mounts had caused criticism from staff officers early in the war who considered this might cause interference during a charge. The image is somewhat at odds with the recruiting poster below.

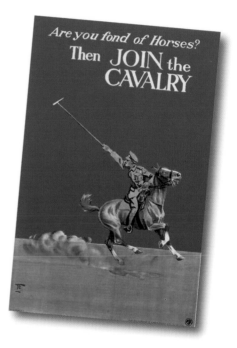

A line of horses, fully equipped, waits at the back of a heavily sandbagged dugout at the entrance to which stand some troopers in a relaxed pose. The photograph reveals just how vulnerable horses were to shellfire, while the men were able to shelter in relative safety. The splintered trees are evidence that this area of the front had been subjected to sustained artillery attack.

three cavalry divisions in the fighting that took place in just two weeks in April 1917 1208 horses were killed or destroyed and a further 749 lost through injury. The horse, to some extent, was making itself obsolescent on the modern battlefield.

During the opening phase of the Battle of the Somme General Seely records taking his Canadian cavalry into an attack in support of an infantry breakthrough, and describes the inevitable and bloody result in the face of sustained and well-directed artillery fire.

Infantry walk among the bodies of horses lying dead at the end of an abortive cavalry attack. The horse's vulnerability to machine gun and artillery fire made scenes such as this inevitable in the early years of the war.

We were just to the right of Fricourt and our infantry in this sector made considerable advance. When I received a message that the infantry had taken two lines of trenches I jumped on to Warrior [his charger] and with one troop rode forward down into the next valley ahead of us. The infantry had just taken the crest of a hill in front. As we

cantered up the side of the valley the infantry in support cheered us to the echo, thinking this was the beginning of the 'great break through'. A shell dropped in the middle of us, and killed one of the orderlies' horses just behind me. Bazentin was wounded in the off foreleg and Antoine's horse in the neck, but both kept going. When we got to the foot of the ridge we found that the infantry were completely held up and that no further advance would be possible. We had suffered few casualties in men and horses, but we were sorely disappointed to have been of so little service.

In the next few weeks it became clear that the cavalry's role in the great battle was effectively nullified, with the horses taking higher casualties than could be sustained.

During the first few weeks of the battle we remained constantly in readiness and I would ride Warrior every day up to the front line to see how matters progressed. One day he was lame and I rode another horse, a chestnut; a chance shell hit him and killed him. I had three ribs broken myself. But after a while it became clear that the cavalry could not be employed, and in our case the horses were sent back far behind the lines with some of the men. The rest of us resumed our places with the infantry.

Weeks earlier, the first appearance of the tank on the battlefield had sustained the belief that cavalry, working alongside these massive, noisy, unreliable mechanical beasts, would come into their own. Seely again:

The original caption to this official war photograph reads 'Cavalrymen resting in a shell hole and waiting for the order to move up.' They are wearing the British 'Brodie' pattern steel helmet, first issued to troops in 1915, and worn by all infantrymen.

Winter on the Western Front. Troops shelter among a group of cavalry horses which have their tails and flanks matted with ice. For the soldiers, the war was, in the words of one observer: 'mud, sleet, ice, mud, noise, jagged steel, mud, horror piled on reeking horror'. Siegfried Sassoon recalled the gradual way in which the role of cavalry horses was reduced: 'The black mare was well bred but had lost the use of one eye. She was now used as a pack pony for carrying ammunition.'

We moved up, three thousand men and horses with our two batteries of artillery, and our own transport and signals and engineers, to a place not far from St Pol. It was here that Warrior and I first saw a tank, then a great secret and carefully guarded. We practised all kinds of manoeuvres, the idea being that the infantry were to break the German front line, and that the cavalry were then to sweep through the gap and take the enemy in the rear. I'm afraid that not many of us who had spent a long time in the trenches, thought that the infantry could break through, or at any rate not until a great force of tanks had been assembled. However we all played up to the part, and did our utmost to get our horses as fit a possible, and well accustomed to machine gun and rifle fire.

The training of horses to perform during the heat and noise of battle was vital to the cavalry's operational usefulness and Seely gives an insight into how a cavalry officer recognised how unnatural it was for a horse to be subjected to the cacophony of the modern battlefield.

He had to endure everything most hateful to him – violent noise, the bursting of great shells and bright flashes at night, when the white light of bursting shells must have caused violent pain to such sensitive eyes as horses possess. Above all, there was the smell of blood, terrifying to every horse. Many people do not realise how acute is his sense of smell, but most will have read of his terror when he smells blood.

Gradually, despite all efforts to maintain itself as a fighting force, the envisaged role of the cavalry on the Western Front was falling into desuetude and by the end of the Battle of the Somme in November 1916 many cavalry chargers were reduced to being beasts of burden having to carry rations, munitions and the general paraphernalia of war to the troops on the front line. Even General Seely's beloved Warrior was not spared the ignominy and dangers of these excursions, as he recalls 'Many times I accompanied these melancholy convoys with Warrior. He too would sometimes sink through the frozen crust into the oozing white mud below, but he was very strong, and when I jumped from his back he would somehow manage to get out, though he had one or two narrow escapes'.

The General describes the plight of other animals less fortunate than his own.

The sombre close of the Battle of the Somme was cruel to horses no less than men. The roads were so completely broken up by alternate frost, snow and rain, that the only way to get ammunition to the forward batteries was to carry it up in panniers slung on horses. Often these poor beasts, who were led forward in long strings with three shells on each side of them, would sink deep into the mud. Sometimes, in spite of all their struggles, they could not extricate themselves, and died where they fell.

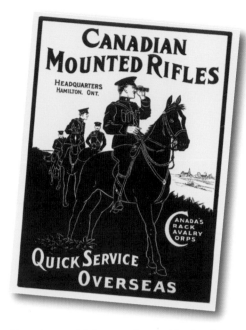

Canada provided men along with the thousands of horses procured from the Dominion during the course of the war. General Seeley, whose memoirs are quoted here, commanded the Canadian Cavalry Brigade while the Canadian Mounted Rifles was an infantry unit of the Canadian Expeditionary Force, one of many former mounted units that gave up their horses, eventually converting to an infantry battalion.

With filthy broken ice edging the war-torn track, this team of six horses pulling an ammunition wagon attempt to make their way through frozen mud hock-deep. As one soldier recalled, any movement became a trial all its own: 'The road was chock full of all kinds of transport and troops all moving to the rear. We mingled with the rest and trudged along at a slow pace for it was hopeless to endeavour to pass anyone or anything, one just had to move with the crowd. Occasionally a horse would stampede, and there would follow a hurried scuffle of troops to keep clear of it.'

Bringing guns and ammunition to the front line was a task that in winter could often only be undertaken by horse transport, and in very trying conditions only by packhorse. Here a troop of cavalry take up ammunition along a track almost impassable to motor transport.

Specialist units such as machine gun crews had panniers specifically adapted for the carriage of the gun and its component parts. Here a horse is shown carrying a Vickers machine gun, tripod and ammunition. The gun itself weighed around 25-30lbs (11-13kg), its tripod 40-50lbs (18-23kg) and ammunition boxes, each of 250 rounds, weighed 22lb (10kg) each. In addition a water container of around a gallon was required in cooling the gun barrel. In all a horse might be expected to carry the weight equivalent to a heavy man, often through deep mud – and often under fire.

There are no figures that accurately record the precise nature of fatalities among horses on the Western Front. Much play has been given to the machine gun but, while it is likely this accounted for high casualties among cavalry units in the early months of the war, once the trench lines became established and the wire firmly in place, general frontal assaults by mounted units were avoided and, while thousands of men were mown down by machine guns, it is unlikely that many horses perished by direct fire in this same way. But, as already mentioned, machine guns were also set up to fire indirectly at previously identified targets from up to 4km in distance resulting in a deadly hail of fire arriving even before the chatter of the gun could be heard by its victims.

A British Vickers machine gun team comprised between six and eight men with the gun and its various components often being carried on horseback. Again this made horse transport a favourite target for alert gunners who would listen out, especially at night, for the telltale sounds of 'iron rimmed wheels and the iron shoes of horses and mules' giving away movement on a particular stretch of road on which their guns had already been trained.

Arthur Russell in *The Machine Gunners* describes one such road leading to the front.

Horses and mules cut up and disembowelled by the exploding of heavy shells also bestrew this highway. As we stumble and stride over these decaying carcases and human bodies some of the men make obscene remarks at their expense, although they know that in all probability they are going to a similar fate.

Nor were the fatalities caused entirely by enemy fire. Misdirected artillery and rounds falling short were a constant hazard to those on the front line, especially during a rolling or creeping barrage which was designed to place a curtain of artillery fire just

Stripped of its equipment but still with its pannier attached a mule lies dead on a snowy track pockmarked with shell holes. Reginald Colwill, fighting with the 2nd Devons, writes 'Night and day, year in year out, the procession of men, wagons, lorries and guns went on, and on, and on, and on. The enemy shelled and bombed the road. Yet miliary policemen stood there on point duty, regulating the traffic. At night a dim, shaded, storm lantern showed where they stood.'

"We could see ammunition wagons trying to replenish getting about half-way to the gun, then a couple of shells would burst blowing the drivers and horses to smithereens, it was a terrible sight but the last two days had made us used to it."

Albert George, Artillery Sergeant.

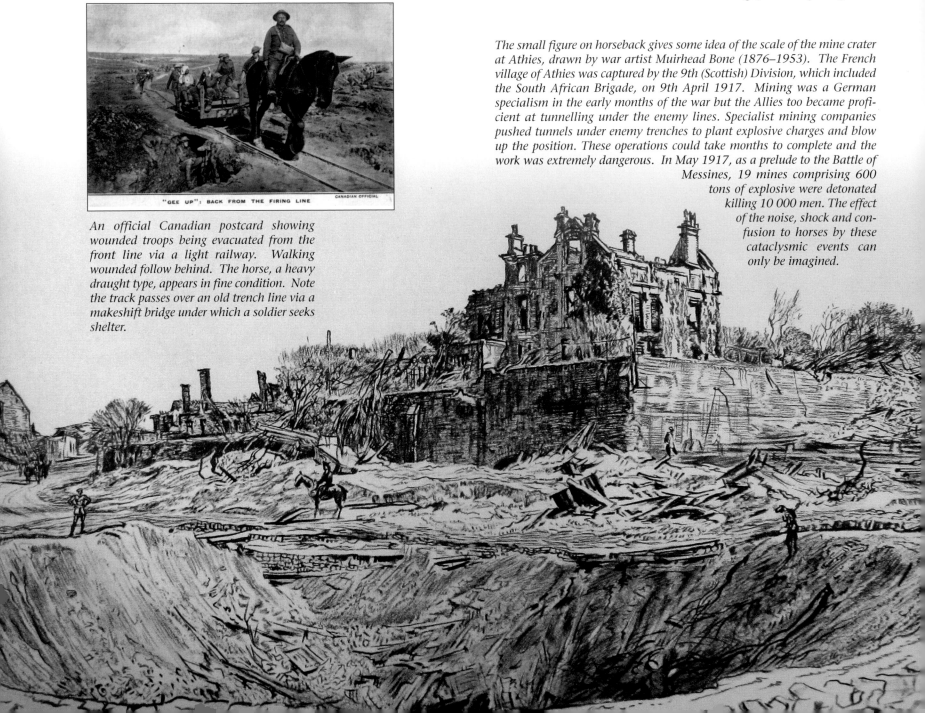

"GEE UP": BACK FROM THE FIRING LINE

CANADIAN OFFICIAL

An official Canadian postcard showing wounded troops being evacuated from the front line via a light railway. Walking wounded follow behind. The horse, a heavy draught type, appears in fine condition. Note the track passes over an old trench line via a makeshift bridge under which a soldier seeks shelter.

The small figure on horseback gives some idea of the scale of the mine crater at Athies, drawn by war artist Muirhead Bone (1876–1953). The French village of Athies was captured by the 9th (Scottish) Division, which included the South African Brigade, on 9th April 1917. Mining was a German specialism in the early months of the war but the Allies too became proficient at tunnelling under the enemy lines. Specialist mining companies pushed tunnels under enemy trenches to plant explosive charges and blow up the position. These operations could take months to complete and the work was extremely dangerous. In May 1917, as a prelude to the Battle of Messines, 19 mines comprising 600 tons of explosive were detonated killing 10 000 men. The effect of the noise, shock and confusion to horses by these cataclysmic events can only be imagined.

Carrying material up to the front lines was often done at night when darkness obscured observation of the roads from the enemy's gunners. Attempts were made to muffle the sounds of harness and wheels but a fearful toll was taken of the troops and horses that made these nightly runs. Here the horses pulling a GS wagon are terrified by the flash of the photographer's camera, the driver attempting to rein them in.

ahead of advancing infantry. Any error in timings led to horrendous casualties among both men and horses.

Accidents with small ordnance were also commonplace:

All through the night, GS wagons bring up more and more boxes of bombs, all sorts and sizes and they have to be sorted somewhere down below. If, as a result of all this manhandling, a pin works loose from one of the Mills type, that's the last we see of it, or its carrier. Some nights are reminiscent of Guy Fawkes, never a dull moment.

While the machine gun and its associated steel web of barbed-wire became, in the public mind at least, the archetypal weapon of death and destruction on the Western Front, in reality it was artillery that became the war's greatest killer, making no distinction between man or animals in its unequivocal destruction. Once the arterial blood of warfare stagnated in the muddy capillaries of the trenches, science stiffened its sinews towards the development of weapons that could kill from afar. As John Terraine has remarked in *White Heat* 'The war of 1914-1918 was an artillery war; artillery was the battle winner, artillery was what caused the greatest loss of life, the most dreadful wounds, and the deepest fear.'

The guns themselves ranged in size from trench mortars that threw small grenade-like bombs into facing enemy positions, to massive railway guns that fired huge shells over great distances. Essentially these weapons fall into two types, cannons that fire a shell over a long arced trajectory and mortars or howitzers that lob a missile over a shorter distance high into the air to land directly on top of its target. Within these types there were different sorts of ammunition designed to have the maximum destructive effect on a given target.

While no such weapon was designed specifically to kill and maim horses they were inevitably part of the daily casualty lists and in many instances suffered more than the troops simply through a greater exposure to artillery fire. While men could shelter in shellholes and trenches, or bury themselves in bunkers, horses simply stood in their makeshift stables, or were tied in the horse lines fully exposed.

At the war's outset most artillery comprised field pieces, such as the famous French '75s' which earned a reputation for their robust quality, rapidity of fire and destructiveness. These smaller weapons were almost exclusively horse drawn.

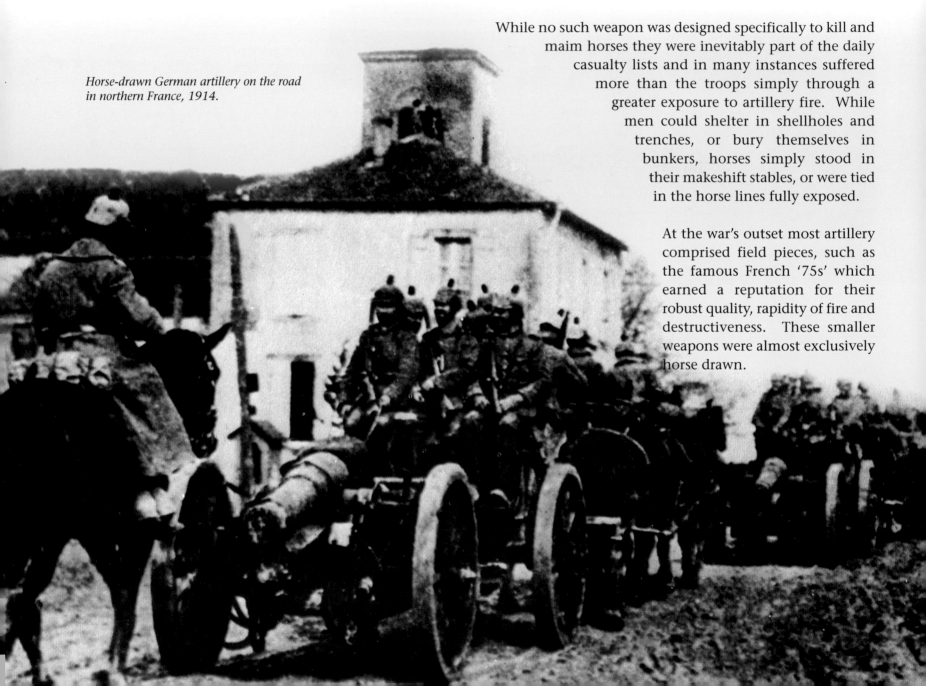

Horse-drawn German artillery on the road in northern France, 1914.

French gunners ready to move out to face the German advance in 1914.

Such guns were designed for defence or attack against opposing forces, infantry or cavalry, their lightness enabling rapid movement around the battlefield. A variety of types of ammunition were available to the gunners dependent upon the target. Shrapnel was favoured for use against infantry and cavalry, a hollow shell, the front of which was packed with steel balls, the rear holding a small explosive charge. The charge could be set to go off while the shell was still in the air, throwing out the steel balls and driving them downwards upon the target. Against densely massed cavalry the effect could be appalling, although the effectiveness was limited against well-drilled troops, as a German officer observed in 1914.

One saw that these dots were infantry advancing, widely extended: English infantry, unmistakably. A field battery on our left had spotted them, and we watched their shrapnel bursting over the advancing line. Soon a second line of dots emerged from the willows along the river bank, at least ten paces apart, and began to advance. More of our batteries came into action; but it was noticed that a shell, however well aimed, seldom killed more than one man, the lines being so well and widely extended.

A British officer describes the effect of shrapnel against a similar attack made by less disciplined German troops.

Poster exhorting Canadians to join a pioneer battalion. Note the implied dangers likely to be faced, shrapnel bursting overhead and aircraft waiting to attack.

The guns lowered their barrels and fired over open sights. That is to say that the Germans were so close that the British did not need to use sights to aim the guns but simply looked down the top of the barrel. They fired shrapnel; in other words the guns were used as giant shotguns, the effect on the Germans being terrible. At this point we decided to withdraw and called up the horse teams to bring out the guns. However the horses could not get up because of fire from the German infantry. The order was given to remove breech blocks, so rendering the guns inoperable, and the gun crews ran for it.

An Austrian 30.5cm howitzer was one of the largest guns of its type used in the First World War

"Every day our defences were levelled. Every night we would crawl out, after long hours spent flat on our stomachs, covered to the neck in mud and blood, and endeavour to repair the damage. Every night we lost a few men, every day we lost a few men."

Thus, while the effect of these smaller calibre guns varied, their reliance upon horses to move them around the field of battle made them vulnerable to capture. As the conflict wore on so bigger and bigger guns were constructed to effect greater destruction at greater distances. This weaponry was specifically designed for purpose and was used at the outset of the set-piece battles to destroy specific targets, to soften up the enemy defences and to wreak havoc among the supply lines leading to the front. Being held further back behind the lines meant they were less likely to be captured, and providing them with ammunition became less hazardous too.

A British 'railway' gun, sited miles behind the front line, could direct shells on to enemy targets 50 miles distant. Shells from these monsters fell at such velocity there was no warning of their arrival.

Guns such as the famous and feared German Paris Gun, nicknamed 'Big Bertha' could hurl a shell weighing 210lbs (94kg) a distance of over eighty miles. Over 20 shells a day from this behemoth rained down on Paris, each reaching an altitude of 25 miles before descending upon the city. A number of such 'railway guns' were used by all sides during the war but, apart from their terror value, in actuality they did little to effect the war's outcome.

More devastating to the troops and horses on the front line were the thousands of medium sized guns and the improvised mortars that were used in daily skirmishes between troops that often were within hailing distance of each another.

By 1916 guns such as this had outgrown the practicality of horse power in moving them from place to place. It was at this time too that the shortage of supply in horses for the Western Front was becoming acute.

By late 1916 the British government was struggling with the dilemma of reserving sufficient horse power on farms to provide the nation's food, and at the same time keeping up numbers of animals for the prosecution of the war. In the absence of any other means, these men are reduced to pulling a massive artillery piece along a narrow gauge railway track. By March 1917 so acute had the supply of horses become that Cabinet minutes record the refusal to expedite the transport of troops from Portugal to the Western Front in favour of resupplying horses from the USA.

The Germans can now throw a bomb 200lbs in weight and 5ft long a distance of 1000 yards, it explodes like a mine and kills by concussion. They sent several over every day and killed a good many. One of the four men of our Battalion who were killed that way I knew quite well, he was the last of five brothers all of whom have been killed in the war.

Mortars were an effective weapon in trench warfare, and much hated. Troops would strain their ears to catch the 'plop!' sound that indicated the firing of an enemy mortar, and consequently take cover. Mortar positions became a favourite target for artillery once their presence was detected and this made them all the more unpopular when sited near one's own trench, for a mortar position would inevitably attract counter-fire.

These weapons were often given humorous or derogatory nicknames by the troops: 'whizz-bangs' (shells fired from light or field artillery which travelled faster than the speed of sound and arrived without warning), 'minnies' (after the German name *minenwerfer*), and 'Jack Johnson's (heavy shells that threw up clouds of black smoke, named after the black American boxer). Humour mitigating their terrifying effect.

One morning, while I was inspecting the rifles of the sentries on duty, I was startled, not to say alarmed, by three whizz-bangs bursting as it seemed all round my head. I heard one coming very close, caught a glimpse of it out of the tail of my eye, and at that moment slipped. I picked myself up, but before I could reach my full height, the minnie burst. A furious hot whirlwind rushed down, seized me and flung me violently back against the earth. I lay half-stunned while a rain of earth and offal pattered down on me, followed by something which whizzed viciously and stuck quivering in the trench wall; it was a piece of jagged steel eighteen inches long.

If caught in the open by shellfire horses and their transports had nowhere to hide, whereas men could at least throw themselves flat to avoid the flying shards of red hot metal. If caught directly by the blast flesh would be literally flayed from bone, and while contemporary diaries record that men did all they could for the screaming and dying animals, their first priority would be to give aid to stricken comrades.

Even when not caught directly by shellbursts, the blast from a heavy shell exploding could blow horses and wagons off the road causing injury and death, while even in those animals uninjured such were the terrifying circumstances that they might bolt pulling fractured wagons and disabled horses along with them.

Panic ensues as shells burst alongside this road in France. Men duck for cover and dive for the shelter of a ditch, while the transport driver attempts to control his horses. In the background, a riderless horse rears in fright.

The original caption to the photograph states 'Pulling out a horse which fell into a ditch where it was blown by the concussion of a big shell-burst. On road to Reutel, Belgium'. Concussion alone was often severe enough to kill men and animals.

A traffic jam formed by American troops making their way to the front line during the Argonne offensive in 1918. Various kinds of transport fill a narrow lane and while these smiling troops are clearly in no immediate danger the scene gives some idea of what might occur should the area come under attack.

It is only through photographs and silent film from that time that we can glimpse the visual horror of these events, and even these static images cannot carry with the them sounds and reeking stench that accompanied such episodes of slaughter and their shocking aftermath.

In his diary a Lieutenant R G Dixon, 14th Battery, Royal Garrison Artillery recalls:

Heaving about in the filthy mud of the road was an unfortunate mule with both of his forelegs shot away. The poor brute, suffering God knows what untold agonies and

terrors, was trying desperately to get to its feet which weren't there. Writhing and heaving, tossing its head about in its wild attempts, not knowing that it no longer had any front legs.

I had my revolver with me, but couldn't get near the animal, which lashed out at us with its hind legs and tossed its head unceasingly. Jerry's shells were arriving pretty fast – we made some desperate attempts to get to the mule so that I could put a bullet behind its ear into the brain, but to no avail.

By lingering there, trying to put the creature out of its pain I was risking not only my life but also my companions'. The shelling got more intense – perhaps one would hit the poor thing and put it out of its misery.

The scene following the shelling of a convoy of supply wagons. Reginald Colwill, fighting with the 2nd Devons, writes 'If a shell knocked out two or three wagons and tore a great hole in the road, the wagons and all there was in them, were buried in it and earth thrown in on top by everybody who could lift a shovel.'

97

A heavy shell falls in the city of Amiens. The Germans bombarded the city from 16 miles away using an artillery piece mounted on a railway track.

Shellfire in towns and cities could have an even more devastating effect than in open country. Confined by the walls of buildings, the shock of explosions was amplified and people and horses were often killed outright by the concussive blast of an exploding shell. Here German officers pass a scene of death and destruction in a captured French town.

With long range gunnery it was possible to throw shells far behind the enemy's lines and at favoured targets including railways and ports, as well as at many of the towns where troop concentrations were known to be quartered.

The incessant shelling brought about other problems for the troops, a phenomenon hitherto unrecognised in warfare, shell shock. As early as 1914 men on the front line began to recognise in their comrades the symptoms associated with the strain of fighting in the trenches, particularly when under an artillery bombardment. But while fighting men saw the effects on their comrades, the authorities were slow to recognise the problem. The symptoms of many sufferers was put down as cowardice and a distressing number of men were shot following courts martial trials; others committed suicide. By the end of the war 80 000 cases were being treated.

While no veterinary report on such trauma appears to exist in respect of horses, there is no reason not to suppose that such sensitive animals, when subjected to similar conditions, should not also have exhibited behaviour alien to their natural state.

"The brisk, merry war to which we have all looked forward for years has taken an unforeseen turn. Troops are murdered with machines, horses have almost become superfluous... The most important people are the engineers... the theories of decades are shown to be worthless."

A German officer writing in 1914.

A German soldier examines dead horses and men, victims of shellfire.

CAUTION

THIS ROAD IS OBSERVED BY THE ENEMY
ALL TRAFFIC MUST GO SLOW
TO AVOID RAISING DUST
WHICH DRAWS ENEMY SHELL FIRE.

M·19895

Troops were continually warned of the dangers of attracting the attention of enemy gunners. The consequences of which could be fatal to both men and horses.

While German gunners listened at night for the sound of horses and wagons, having zeroed in their heavy guns on particular stretches of road, their airmen also saw the value in attacking horse-drawn convoys. Frank Dunham in *The Long Carry* makes the interesting observation regarding enemy aircraft of which he says 'It was common talk that the enemy preferred to drop bombs on the horse lines rather than on camps, as he considered horses more difficult to replace than men.'

There are other reports of pilots on both sides targeting transport columns. This would have made sense both strategically and from a pragmatic viewpoint in terms of effecting the greatest damage at the least danger to the aircraft. Long lines of men, wagons and horses on a straight and open road made the perfect target from the slow moving gun platform of these early fighters.

Even the sensitive Cecil Lewis, the writer who went on to co-found the BBC, showed no mercy when it came to shooting up a German supply wagon from the air.

On the main road from Bapaume to Pozières, five miles beyond the line, we saw two horse-drawn limbers. They were coming up at the gallop, bringing ammunition to their batteries, their six horses stretching out, the riders crouching low over their necks, the wagon rolling and swaying on the awful road. We dived. At a thousand feet Pip opened fire with the Lewis gun. Whether he killed or wounded the leading horse of the first limber I shall never know. Perhaps it was just

Old technology meets new. A crashed British aircraft, an RE-8, is passed by a horse-drawn GS wagon.

panic; but the horse crumpled up, and the others with their tremendous momentum, overran him, and the whole lot piled up in the ditch, a frenzied tangle of kicking horses, wagons and men. The second limber, following close behind the first, swerved, but could not avoid its leader; its wagons overturned, wheels spinning and split. Shells rolled over the road. We returned elated. We had helped to win the war.

The display of large red crosses on ambulances were echoed in flags flown over the other front line medical bases and were supposed to offer some protection from aerial and other attacks. Captain Hampton recalls in his diary 'We flew our flags, a Red Cross and a Union Jack, but we were the only unit I saw on Redan Hill to do this.'

And aircraft posed another threat beyond that of direct attack; they served as spotters for the artillery, directing precise fire on detected movements of troops and on key positions. Hampton reports on a meeting with a wounded officer:

'Erecting Aeroplanes' a drawing by war artist Muirhead Bone (1876-1953). The war saw the rapid development of aircraft by both sides and although, as in this picture, the machines look primitive, they were in fact at the cutting edge of technology, providing support for attacks on the enemy and vital aerial reconnaissance.

Possibly a faked photograph of a German plane attacking a tank watched by a small group of German soldiers. By 1916, with the gradual appearance of more and more mechanised weaponry on the battlefield, the last rites the horse as a meaningful way of waging war were being read.

A recruitment poster for the Canadian Army tellingly superimposes a rearing motorcycle over the background image of a knight on horseback. Machines and not horses now symbolised the future of battlefield power.

This officer says he thinks his guns were lost for certain, as they could not get them out of action, their horses nearly all being killed. He seemed to think the same thing was happening in other parts of our line. He was perfectly astounded by the way an aeroplane was spotting and range finding for the German gunners. He knew nothing about the infantry except that things were not good.

While mud became the leitmotif of those who wrote about the Great War – a stinking quagmire of rain-filled shellholes infested with vermin and pervaded by a stench of death – the roads behind the front lines offered a hell all their own.

Targeted by aircraft, given special attention by enemy artillery, these arteries witnessed the terrible toll of horses which, as compassionate as their drivers might be, could not be spared under the pressure to deliver ammunition and food to the troops in the front line, or to transport seriously wounded men to hospitals in the rear. In *A Call to Arms,* Joseph Murray describes one such road:

THE WAR HORSES

The journey to the rear was a nightmare. There was no shelter at all over the newly captured open ground. The road to Beaucourt was a graveyard of many of the ration parties that had attempted to get through to us. Dixies that once held that much needed precious hot stew were perforated and scattered all over the place, intermingled with broken boxes of ammunition, picks and shovels. When we reached the village it was a dreadful sight: mutilated bodies of men, horses and mules everywhere among which we had to shelter while waiting a chance to run the gauntlet around a spot known to us as 'suicide corner'. The road, the only one, and the only way in or out of the area of our attack, had been in enemy hands for years and now they were free to concentrate all their fire on this narrow strip of activity.

French artillerymen in the Vosges forest in 1915 pose alongside their somewhat anti-quated gun pulled by a caterpillar tractor.

By the time the war was into its third year the shortage of horses was becoming acute. The high attrition rates were exacerbated by the transportation compromises over whether horses and their feedstuffs should have priority over munitions and other material. Shipping losses due to the submarine menace in the Atlantic had reached dangerous levels; in the first three months of 1917 Britain lost 470 vessels to torpedoes leaving her with fewer than six weeks' supplies of food in hand. Throughout the war calls were made for economies in the use of horses, Prime Minister Asquith calling upon the army to curb their spending; after all, he said (presumably speaking of the cavalry) 'Horses had played an unexpectedly small part in this war'. By 1916 Kitchener ordered the appointment of a Committee to report on ways in which the reliance upon horses might be controlled, and they in turn reduced the amount of shipping available for army remounts. Even so, in 1917, the stock of animals in use by the military rose to 870 000 from 535 000 in 1915.

The falling graph charting the problems associated with the supply of horses for the war, and the dilemma of growing or importing feed for them instead of for the human population, had, by 1917, converged with the rising need for mechanical vehicles to help offset the shortage of horses in agriculture. Much exercised by these problems the British government, just as they had done for horses, looked to North America for aid in providing tractors and ploughs. In March 1917, in a report to the Food Production Department, a gloomy picture is painted.

It has been ascertained that there is a total of 459 tractors of various makes on order of which 35 are expected to Dock at Liverpool on the 4th inst. The actual number of tractors already bought and already in use is 32.

A month later the news is not much better, as a report to the War Cabinet in April 1917 makes clear.

The provision of tractors and ploughs is a much more anxious matter. Owing to shipping and other difficulties the importation of American machinery has been exceedingly disappointing. Of the 600 tractors and 214 ploughs ordered only 78 tractors and 108 ploughs have been delivered.

The same Cabinet report suggests that production of American tractors under licence in Britain would be one way to solve this difficulty: an idea that arises from a not entirely selfless suggestion by British industry:

The only solution, so far as the bulk of supply is concerned, appears, therefore, to be to develop the suggestions made by a group of British motor manufacturers that they should combine resources to produce a replica of the Ford tractor, which is extremely simple, and cheap, and has proved its practical value after a severe and extended trial.

Thus a suggestion, taken up to solve a wartime crisis, had a longer term effect. The widespread and urgent introduction to the farmer of cheap mechanical power did much to speed driving horse power from the land in the decades following the war's end.

An early tractor pulls a binder during harvest at Blofield, Norfolk, in 1920.

THE WAR HORSES

What would almost certainly have taken several teams of horses to accomplish, this Holt tractor is able to do alone. Here the tractor is towing three wagons hauling the gun barrel, a limber, and the main gun assembly. The early advantage of horses over wheeled mechanical vehicles on poor ground was, by 1917, overcome by the introduction of caterpillar tracks, although the work on making the roadway passable shown in the photograph indicates that a reasonable surface was still required.

With acute food shortages at home exacerbated by the shortages of horses, and continual demands for more horse power at the front, a crisis was looming. On the Home Front companies previously involved in the production of motor vehicles were urged to move towards war work, filling their factories with female labour which, often to the surprise of the captains of industry, proved just as efficient if not more so than their male counterparts. On the land too women filled the gap left by those engaged in the fighting and the formation of the Women's Land Army in 1915 formalised the development of this huge pool of labour. By 1917 a quarter of a million women were at work on the land, 20 000 of which were members of the WLA.

The advantages of major wars is never lost on industrialists and in America, as in Britain, many companies turned production over to the machinery of war. The Holt Tractor Company, forerunner of the present day Caterpillar Inc., took up the patent for producing a tractor with caterpillar tracks from the British company, Hornsby,

who invented the idea in 1905. Holt demonstrated one of their vehicles to the British Army early in the war and several were ordered specifically for use in hauling large pieces of artillery. It was from witnessing the success of these vehicles in France that Major Ernest Swinton, a war correspondent on the Western Front, got the idea for a tracked fighting vehicle. Within a year he had convinced Winston Churchill of the soundness of his idea from which the tank was developed.

The advent of the tank was a weapon that, as far as champions of the cavalry were concerned, laid to rest many of the long-held beliefs that this elite arm had yet an important part to play. But there remained the hope, and belief, that a breakthrough achieved by the use of massed tanks would open the door to a mobile mounted force chasing and mopping up the enemy.

But it was a forlorn hope at best. Tanks, first introduced in battle in 1916, were inefficient, unreliable, hellish for their crews to work in, and susceptible to counter attacks by grenades, artillery and the recently introduced flamethrower. They were also a novel weapon and the best way of how to use them in battle was little understood by the generals, resulting in a battlefield debut that was ignominious, when even the tank's considerable potential shock value on opposing forces was wasted.

'A Dead Tank' - a charcoal sketch by war artist Muirhead Bone (1876-1953). During the Battle of Cambrai, in a little over two weeks the Allies lost 176 tanks, a third of the number deployed, either through enemy action, breakdowns, or through 'ditching'. The Germans found the tank particularly susceptible to concentrated artillery fire, a fate suffered by the tank in this sketch.

Troopers rush forward to assist their comrades after an attack by a cavalry unit. Of the horses returning many are riderless. In the face of modern weaponry the cavalry were likely to suffer high casualties.

"Aeroplanes and tanks are only accessories to the man on a horse"

Sir Douglas Haig

'Tank' - a charcoal sketch by war artist
Muirhead Bone (1876-1953).

THE WAR HORSES

A few months before the massed tank attack at Cambrai, the Allies attempted a breakthrough at Arras in April 1917. In this attack only 11 tanks took part in the battle but the cavalry were on hand to exploit any breakthrough. In this photograph a platoon moves up to the line passing a Field Artillery battery of 18 pounders. A tank stands in the background and a line of cavalry beyond. Despite early gains on the first day of the battle no breakthrough came and the British casualties alone totalled 150 000.

General Seely, commanding the Canadian Cavalry Brigade, describes in his book *My Horse Warrior* the prelude to the first great tank battle at Cambrai in November 1917.

No long afterwards, I was told, as a great secret, of the proposed mass tank attack on Cambrai. Yet again they told me, my brigade was to have the honour of leading the advance. The secret was so well kept that even the Cabinet at home did not know of the impending attack, and when it happened it came as a complete surprise, not only to His Majesty's Ministers, but to the Germans in that sector.

But in spite of all the secrecy and high hopes, Seely's optimism was short lived and his cavalry supporting the tanks suffered heavily.

For a few hours it was a glorious success. It was fine to be cantering along just behind a tank into the village of Masniéres. Down the main street we went, Warrior's nose nearly touching the tank as it reached the bridge over the Canal l'Escaut. Then misfortune befell the adventure for with a frightful bang the bridge collapsed and the tank fell through into the canal. Warrior and I nearly fell in too, but we just avoided it. There was a good deal of rifle fire going on and many of the horses behind us were hit.

It was at Cambrai that tanks were first used in significant numbers; 476 in total, accompanied by six divisions of infantry and two of cavalry, the latter 'to exploit any breakthrough'. But once the Germans overcame their initial surprise, in the ensuing days their alarm rapidly turned to disdain for the new wonder weapon. Not only were tanks a large enough target on which to concentrate machine gun and light artillery fire, the fact that they continually broke down meant they often became sitting ducks.

Despite their dubious record in battle, tanks were generally admired by the troops who welcomed anything that might make attacks on the enemy positions more successful at less risk to themselves. This male tank appeared, along with a handful of others, at the opening of the Battle of the Somme in September 1916. These 'Landships' were indeed at the cutting edge of military technology – the scientists' answer to creating mobility in a war that, robbed of the traditional fluidity that cavalry brought to the battlefield, had become gridlocked.

By 1918 tanks had become an essential component of warfare on the Western Front. From now on it was technology and science that were to rule the battlefield and it was not long before cavalry regiments revolved around armoured cars and tanks – not horses. Here a group of four tanks warrant hardly a glimpse from the soldiers who wait on the St Quentin Canal before the battle in September 1918.

Their indifferent performance has been given as a reason why the Germans delayed the introduction of their own tanks, but by early 1917 they too began to use tanks in battle. These were at first no better than the Allied vehicles but nonetheless effective enough against any kind of mounted attack across open ground, a tactic still envisaged by the proponents of cavalry; although there appears to be no record of cavalry being directly engaged against tanks. Even so, against this new weapon, whether the tank was employed as a means of enabling cavalry to carry an attack *to* the enemy, or in preventing such an attack *by* the enemy, the horse would lose out either way.

But if the tank largely represented an indirect threat to the horse the First World War saw the introduction of a yet more lethal and pernicious weapon, deadly to man and horse alike: poison gas.

As with artillery, horses were particularly vulnerable to gas attack, having little to protect them from the awful effects of the various types of gas employed. When the gas alarm sounded soldiers naturally first looked to save themselves, sheltering in deep bunkers behind anti-gas curtains which helped restrict the poisonous ingress. Horses took their chances above ground and suffered accordingly.

Types of gas varied in their effect. While figures suggest around 4 per cent (100 000) of combat deaths were due to gas, many of the soldiers who were exposed non-lethally suffered lifetime damage both physically and emotionally. Its relatively poor performance as a weapon of war was offset by the fear it caused, especially among those who witnessed the torment of fellow soldiers afflicted by it. The insidious nature of the silent clouds drifting across the desolate battlefield filled onlookers with a palpable portent of horror.

We had a new man at the periscope, on this afternoon in question; I was sitting on the fire step, cleaning my rifle, when he called out to me: 'There's a sort of greenish, yellow cloud rolling along the ground out in front, it's coming...' But I waited for no more, grabbing my bayonet, which was detached from the rifle, I gave the alarm by banging

As one soldier, remarking on poison gas, put it 'It's the animals that suffer the most, the horses, mules, cattle, dogs, cats, they having no helmets to save them.'

Clouds of poison gas head from the network of German trenches towards the Allied lines in 1917. Subject to the vagaries of the weather, gas was limited in its effectiveness as a battlefield weapon, but for many horses, unable to escape its pernicious effect, it spelt death or months of misery in veterinary care.

While it was the French who instigated the use of chemical weapons in the First World War, the Germans were the first to employ poison gas on a large scale. Here a German soldier leads a team of horses all of them wearing gas masks.

an empty shell case, which was hanging near the periscope. At the same instant, gongs started ringing down the trench, the signal for Tommy to don his respirator, or smoke helmet, as we call it. Gas travels quietly, so you must not lose any time; you generally have about eighteen or twenty seconds in which to adjust your gas helmet. For a minute, pandemonium reigned in our trench – Tommies adjusting their helmets, bombers running here and there, and men turning out of the dugouts with fixed bayonets, to man the fire step.

German gas is heavier than air and soon fills the trenches and dugouts, where it has been known to lurk for two or three days. A company man on our right was too slow in getting on his helmet; he sank to the ground, clutching at his throat, and after a few spasmodic twistings, went West. It was horrible to see him die, but we were powerless to help him. In the corner of a traverse, a little, muddy cur dog, one of the company's pets, was lying dead, with his two paws over his nose.

It's the animals that suffer the most, the horses, mules, cattle, dogs, cats, they having no helmets to save them. At times, gas has been known to travel, with dire results, fifteen miles behind the lines.

By 1915 the Germans were using chlorine gas on a large scale and experiments were being made as to the best method of countering this and other chemical agents. At

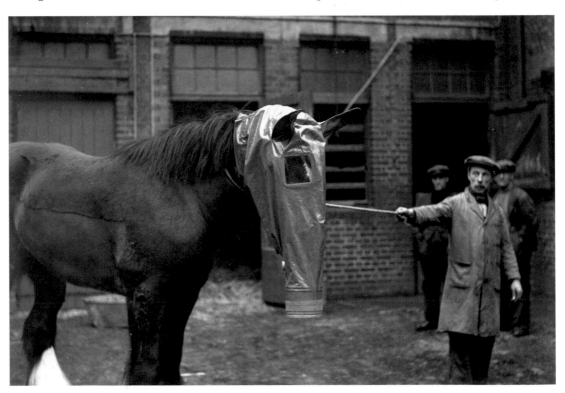

After its first use on the battlefield, the importance of providing horses with protection from poison gas was quickly realised and experiments were made with several types of gas mask using a variety of materials.

first men were issued with simple cotton pads that had to be pressed over the mouth. Later developments saw the pads impregnated with a chemical solution to counter the effects of gas, and the British Hypo Helmet introduced in June 1915 covered the whole head and was made of a chemical absorbing fabric with a built-in eye piece. By April 1916 the box respirator became standard issue for British troops. At the same time there were experiments undertaken for the production of gas masks for horses and these too became standard issue throughout the British Army.

Chlorine gas had much the same effect on horses as it did on the men. If breathed in in sufficient volume it could be fatal, destroying lung tissue through the formation of hydrochloric acid when combined with the water in the lungs. In smaller doses the effects could be agonising and the cumulative trauma could lead to hypoxia due to the depletion of oxygen and eventual heart failure. Treatment, where possible, would include bathing the horse's eyes with a saline solution and washing the animal with copious amounts of soap and water.

Generally gas was released from cylinders but could also be delivered via explosive chemical shells. Being heavier than air, chlorine gas tended to creep close to the ground, accumulating in shell holes and trenches. Men who lay in the bottom of the trench to escape, and wounded men unable to rise from their stretchers, suffered more than those who remained on the firestep. Unless they were in a hollow, stabled animals also avoided the worst effects of chlorine gas.

Edwin Noble, a corporal at No.8 Veterinary Hospital in France, captured in this charcoal and watercolour drawing the damage caused to this horse afflicted by mustard gas.

Experiments using gas as a weapon continued on all sides, with even more deadly types being introduced, including phosgene and mustard gas. Phosgene was most deadly of all, accounting for 85 per cent of all human deaths through gas attack. There was little that could be done to save the animals afflicted; while bottled oxygen was on hand to help treat soldiers, it was not available for the immediate treatment of horses.

Mustard gas caused the most terrible suffering to anything that fell victim to it, man or beast. A blister agent, it caused severe skin and eye pain and irritation, the chemical burns resulting in huge blisters on any part of the body which had come into contact with the gas. Moreover, the gas attached itself to plants and where it lay in the soil, that too could remain active for weeks – a particular problem for grazing animals.

Gas mask drill. These artillery horses have canvas bags attached to their bridle cheek pieces from which the gas masks can be quickly withdrawn.

This chapter has looked at the principal means by which horses became casualties in the First World War, the conditions under which they were daily asked to perform their duties, and the gradual process by which their perceived importance to the military was reduced as the technology of war advanced. In the following chapter we look at the care of horses as practised by the British military authorities, and the vast infrastructure required to support their vital role in the war.

The Pity of War

Setting aside for a moment the moral issues concerning war and the maniacal politics that drew the world into senseless slaughter in 1914, we can only be left to wonder at the superb organisation that oversaw, not only the requisition and purchase of animals for the war, but their safe transport, training and ultimately their veterinary care. In theory, and ignoring the benefit granted to us through hindsight, bearing in mind the restrictions, largely financial, imposed by politicians on the military commanders, the British Army left almost nothing to chance in this regard. In practice officers of every branch carried a *Field Service Pocket Book* which advised them, among many other things, on matters related to the treatment and care of horses.

It is worth reflecting for a moment on the numbers of horses involved throughout the war, taking into account that in this book we are almost exclusively looking at the British Army on the Western Front. The subtitle of this book refers to the death of a million horses, a number which includes the total losses among those animals owned by the civilian population and the combined Allied armies on the Western Front, of which the French Army alone lost almost 542 000.

Desolation: horses lying dead alongside a GS wagon where the body of a soldier lies.

It is estimated that the total number of horses mules and donkeys killed on all sides and in all theatres of war between 1914 and 1918 was 8 million – a million fewer than the total estimated human military casualties – while 2.5 million horses had been treated in veterinary hospitals, of which 2 million had been restored successfully enough for the animal to return to duty. During the course of the war the British Army on the Western Front had 256 000 horses killed (558 000 British soldiers died in same theatre). The British Army Veterinary Corps hospitals treated 725,000 horses in France over the course of the war, successfully healing around 520 000. World-wide 2.5 million animals were treated by the AVC, 80 per cent being returned to duty.

Lessons from earlier wars, in particular the Boer War where the annual wastage rate had risen as high as 67 per cent, saw a massive improvement in the overall treatment of horses in the First World War during which the British Army lost 15 per cent of its animals either killed in battle, dying from some other cause, missing or abandoned.

The main responsibility for the care of horses in the British Army fell on the shoulders of the Royal Army Veterinary Corps which had its beginnings in the Army Veterinary Service, formed in 1796. At that time the AVS was largely occupied with cavalry mounts although much of what was learned about the treatment and care of animals on active service by them was invaluable to those involved in later wars. In 1914 the AVS became the Army Veterinary Corps (its Royal prefix being granted in 1918), and when the BEF embarked for France, 122 AVC officers and 797 other ranks went with them. Their job was to look after 53 000 horses.

On the home front organisations such as the RSPCA held regular events in support of animals serving with the armed forces.

A team of twelve horses haul a GS wagon across churned up ground beside a temporary cemetery containing a variety of markers. Crude little stakes mark some burials, while a shovel thrown to one side lies waiting for fresh graves to be dug.

However much had been learned from earlier experiences in war, the conflict on the Western Front threw up challenges never before faced by those in the AVC, whose work is looked at more closely later in this chapter. The weaponry, the blasted landscape of trenches and acres of barbed wire, presented endless opportunities for horses to fall ill or get injured. As anyone knows who owns a horse, if it can find a way of injuring itself, it will.

Men of the 4th Essex Battalion transport company prepare to leave for France in 1914. In action and in the ubiquitous muddy conditions it could take up to twelve hours to clean horses and their harnesses. If this work was not done both equipment and horse would quickly become unserviceable.

Nor did the injury need to be caused by enemy action, the severe conditions at the front, and the workload required of animals gave rise to problems that required immediate treatment. Travis Hampson MC records a typical event with the BEF in 1914:

> *I saw the transport off and then had to wait in the town for a man leading a sick horse. The horse kept lying down and was only got up again with great difficulty. I think it was colic. I had nothing to give it, and there was no vet to be had of course, and I was a bit uncertain what to do. I wouldn't have him ill-treated, and didn't like to shoot him. After getting him along about a mile I found a stable attached to some works, and put him*

in there. There was only an old Frenchman in charge, who wasn't a bit pleased, especially as I made the ASC driver make him up a good bed with the straw belonging to the place. This was the best I could do, so we just left him.

Familiar problems such as saddle sores quickly became acute and, if not soon treated, rendered an animal unfit for service. Travis Hampson again:

I had to give up riding my nag later in the day and footslog. It was devilish hot too. A small saddle gall had broken down again in spite of any adjustment the saddler could make or different foldings of the saddle blanket. I think it was really due to his bad habit mentioned earlier of being constantly on the jog. He would not walk march even at the end of our long treks, so it was no use trying to tire him out of it.

For men and horses on the march the question of finding food and shelter was vital if the animals were to be kept in reasonable shape. This meant finding a billet before nightfall otherwise the men would be left to bivouac and the horses to stand in the lines.

A bombed out building serves as a rough temporary shelter for these horses waiting to take ammunition up to the front. While such ruins affording some protection, the vulnerability of horses in the face of shelling is obvious.

We arrived there with no billets available except one small school. The horses had to stand in the pouring rain all night harnessed up. It was a beastly night – pitch dark when we got in. There was just room in a small bedroom for our valises to be unrolled, but we were glad to be under a roof of any sort.

Close to the front lines the stabling for horses was rudimentary and sometimes non-existent, and in such primitive accommodation the care that could be provided was basic and the health of the animals could quickly deteriorate. Even the smallest structure visible above ground became a target for enemy artillery or aerial attack with dire consequences as recorded by Lieutenant Wheatley in his book *Officer and Temporary Gentleman*.

When the bombs had ceased falling we went over to see what damage had been done. I saw my first dead man twisted up beneath a wagon where he had evidently tried to take shelter; but we had not sustained many human casualties. The horses were another matter. They were dead ones lying all over the place and score of others were floundering and screaming with broken legs, terrible neck wounds or their entrails hanging out. We went back for our pistols and spent the next hour putting the poor, seriously injured brutes out of their misery by shooting them through the head. To do this we had to wade ankle deep through blood and guts. That night we lost over 100 horses.

What is described in the original caption to the photograph as 'an active service stable' reveals a good deal about the extreme conditions in which the horses lived. There is snow on the ground and the only shelter for a few of the horses is a low stand of corrugated iron at the far side of which is erected a primitive manger for hay. Two of the horses eat from nose bags while the soldier on the left attempts to curry comb another. The ribs clearly stand out on the horse in the centre, indicating the paucity of their diet.

THE WAR HORSES

'A Stable on the Western Front' a drawing by war artist Muirhead Bone (1876-1953). This remarkable building, perhaps a hangar for an airship, has been taken over as a makeshift stable by a cavalry regiment.

Not all stables were of such makeshift quality and the magnificent building taken over by the cavalry in Muirhead Bone's lively sketch is in startling contrast to the ramshackle stables shown on the previous page.

Care of the animals' feet was a constant problem. While shoeing was largely left to the farriers supporting each regiment and those of the AVC, the ever-changing but constantly atrocious roads and tracks near the front played havoc with sensitive hooves and once such a condition became chronic the horse was *hors de combat*, some-

times fatally so. A further challenge was the deliberate spreading of caltrops, four-pronged metal spikes that when scattered always left one spike pointing upwards. Used since Roman times as an effective anti-personnel weapon, they were particularly feared by the cavalry as they were almost impossible to spot until too late, and delivered crippling injuries. Early in the war, while cavalry remained a significant threat, both sides constructed a variety of similar weapons intended to prevent or deter cavalry attacks.

The random spread of sharp metal around the battlefield, rusting wire, shrapnel, discarded nails and tins, made travel through mud and water a perilous enterprise for man and beast.

These engineers have been removing spiked boards from a roadway leading to the German lines. Laid early in the war to prevent cavalry approaching, these ugly metal spikes could deal crippling injuries to a horse. In other areas individual spikes, caltrops, would be spread around randomly, one point always facing upwards.

Firewood, particularly in winter, was always at a premium near the front lines and soldiers would take any opportunity to scrounge timber. But their foraging came at a price for horses, with 500 injured each week on this one stretch of road by discarded nails, as this notice spells out.

This detritus of war also provided hidden dangers when it found its way into hay and other foodstuffs. The near miss that almost spelt the end of General Seeley's charger, Warrior, was not a random incident.

> *Anyone who has never seen a powerful thoroughbred suffering from internal pain can have no conception of the terrible sight. The energy of those wonderful muscles, which enable him to jump six feet in the air, is used in the most fantastic and fearful contortions in the endeavour to dislodge the cause of the pain. Warrior was leaping about in this battered horse box like a mad thing. To escape his violence I climbed on to a beam. Meantime a veterinary officer clambered on to the beam with me and told me he knew what was wrong. Warrior had swallowed a piece of sharp metal, shaped like a crooked nail, with his hay. There had been several cases of it and most of the horses had died.*

Thankfully Warrior survived but there is no doubt that accidents such as these put paid to many horses, over and above the thousands who were victims of the intentional havoc wrought by bullets and bombs.

As the 'Kindness to Animals' sign on the previous page indicates, it can be implied from this and many other contemporary records that soldiers reserved a particularly sympathy for horses that were killed and injured. For many it was a specific obligation, reaching beyond that empathy naturally held for their fighting comrades – a recognition perhaps that this was a war begun and fought, however reluctantly, by men of free will, and that horses, 'dumb animals' in the most caring sense, were wholly innocent victims.

A memoir by Gunner, H. Doggett, writing in 1917, helps to illustrate this.

> *Our ammunition wagon had only been there a second or two when a shell killed the horse under the driver. We went over to him and tried to unharness the horse and cut the traces away. He just kneeled and watched this horse.*
>
> *A brigadier then came along, a brass hat, and tapped this boy on the shoulder and said, 'Never mind, sonny!' The driver looked up at him for a second and all of a sudden he said, 'Bloody Germans!' Then he pointed his finger and he stood like stone as though he was transfixed.*
>
> *The Brass Hat said to his captain, 'All right, take the boy down the line and see that he has two or three days rest.' Then he turned to our captain and said, 'If everyone was like that who loved animals we would be all right.'*

Back at home these feelings translated themselves into a rather more sentimental effusions, artists in particular producing paintings that showed the war horse as exemplifying honour and power – an echo of earlier times and containing many of the traditional elements of nineteenth century art, and earlier. But there was, in Europe particularly, a growth of movements away from these traditions, and these included the Cubists, the Vorticists, the Futurists, and Expressionism which had its origins in Germany before the outbreak of war. Sculpture too was breaking free of convention and one of the most powerful works from this time is le Grand Cheval (The Large Horse) constructed in 1914 by the French artist Raymond Duchamp-Villon. Perhaps no other artwork embodies so well all the elements of equine genius combined with a dynamic mechanical power; a perfect embodiment of the horse and modern war. The artist became a victim of the war after enlisting as a medical officer in a cuirassier regiment, where he became an expert horseman. In 1916 he contracted typhoid fever which led to his early death in 1918.

'Dies Irae' by Maxfield Parrish (1870-1966). Parrish, an American, achieved great popularity around the time of the First World War. This painting first appeared in King Albert's Book *published at Christmas 1914 in support of the Belgian Fund.*

But among the most popular works of the day was a painting by an Italian artist Fortunino Matania, a professional illustrator who worked for the major magazines of the day including the *Sphere* and the *Graphic*. Matania illustrated many major events of the Edwardian period, the era before high quality photographs could be printed.

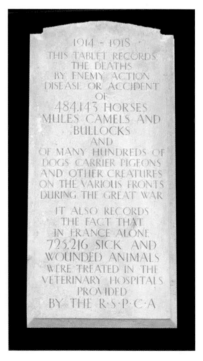

On the outbreak of the war, Matania became a war artist on the staff of the *Sphere*, his graphic illustrations of trench life enjoying public acclaim. But his painting for the Blue Cross organisation, titled 'Goodbye Old Man' became his most famous work, adored by a public drawn to its obvious appeal. It shows a British soldier nursing the head of his dying horse while shells burst around him and a comrade calls out for him to leave. The image was used by many of the organisations whose work was devoted to the care of animals in wartime including the American Red Star and the Blue Cross, to whom the original painting was gifted.

Non combatants in both Britain and America were keen to do all they could to support their 'boys' at the front. Thousands were engaged in pursuits ranging from knitting gloves and balaclavas to the collection of moss and spider webs for use in the treatment of wounds. Much of this volunteer effort went towards the care of horses and among the many organisations involved were The Dumb Friends League, The Blue Cross Fund, the American Red Star and the RSPCA. Each had their own terms of reference but worked towards a common aim; the care of animals used in the war. As is still true today, fund raising for animal welfare has always found a supportive public, and great work is done through the money raised.

The RSPCA, the world's oldest animal welfare charity, gave direct support to the armed forces through many of their employees joining up in 1914, a number being recruited into the AVC. Thereafter funds raised, in excess of £250 000, paid for training manuals, horse ambulances and other material help for the AVC, and by 1915 over 50 per cent of RSPCA staff were serving with the armed forces.

Fortunino Matania's painting 'Goodbye Old Man' came to be an iconic image for those involved in animal welfare during the First World War, appearing on posters for a variety of charitable organisations. Opposite: This tablet is to be found at the RSPCA WWI Memorial Dispensary in London, paying tribute to the animals killed in the war and commemorating the work done by the RSPCA in treating the injured.

Similarly, the American Humane Association, founded in 1877, eagerly stepped in when, in 1917, it was asked by the US War Department to provide help. This led to the inception of The American Red Star Relief programme which largely looked to the welfare of the 250 000 mules and horses serving with the US forces. They played a major part in treating, it is estimated,

68 000 animals each month. This branch of the AHA is active today under the name Red Star Emergency Services.

In a somewhat purple passage by W. Scarth Dixon, writing in the *Graphic* in January 1915, he describes the achievements of these charitable organisations on the Western Front.

Many of the horses have had successful bullet and shell extractions, and everything is done to alleviate their sufferings, and to cure the wounded as quickly and efficaciously as possible so as to get them back to the ranks. Besides providing comfortable and sanitary stabling, the Blue Cross has rented meadows quite near the stables, so that invalids may get out to graze and exercise and enjoy the fresh air and any gleams of sunshine vouchsafed. There, with the sound of guns not far distant, they may dream for a little space of the old peaceful days at home, and recover their nerve for future activity.

The Blue Cross charity sprang out of Our Dumb Friends League, founded in 1897 and which, in the First World War, also dedicated itself to the welfare of animals, providing veterinary supplies and supporting hospitals. It too remains a leading light in animal welfare today.

Spanish officers visit a veterinary hospital on the Western Front. The original caption suggests the horse has had its front left foreleg amputated and, while this procedure is unusual, it is quite possible for a horse to survive on three legs with a prosthesis fitted. Throughout the war, surgeons called upon to treat badly injured soldiers in vast numbers used their skills in taking forward the surgical processes related to amputations, working with specialists in the development of prosthetic limbs. Veterinary surgeons too would naturally have looked to increase their knowledge and skill in helping their equine patients.

BLUE + FUND

President : LADY SMITH-DORRIEN.   Chairman : SIR ERNEST FLOWER.

Hon. Treasurer : GENERAL SIR LESLIE RUNDLE, G.C.B.

TO HELP
HORSES IN WAR TIME
ALSO
HOSPITALS FOR WAR DOGS
IRRESPECTIVE OF NATIONALITY.

ARTHUR J. COKE, Secretary, 59 Victoria Street, London, S.W. 1.

As far as the Army was concerned the support from these charities, and others, was channelled through the AVC. Although this unit of the army started the war modestly in terms of numbers it quickly became key in maintaining the supply of horse power vital to the effectiveness of the fighting troops.

An article published in *The War Illustrated*, a magazine that continued in publication throughout the period 1914–1918 underlines the importance of charities in assisting the work of the AVC.

At the numerous places where the A.V.C. horse hospitals are situated help of various kinds is always needed. I can assure all those who subscribed in answer to the Duke of Portland's appeal on behalf of the R.S.P.C.A. Fund that nothing could be of more benefit to horses at the front than this fund. The Society, is the only one recognised and authorised by the Army Council to collect funds for our horses with the armies. Its aim is to augment the supply of horse hospitals, horse shelters, medical stores, hospital and stable requisites – such as rugs, woollen bandages, head collars, halters – and to

An officer directs the loading of horses into a horse box in France c.1915. The two animals on the left have bandages on their legs suggesting that, having had treatment, they are on their way to recuperate. Each animal is marked with various letters and numbers no doubt related to their origin, and perhaps to their medical records.

provide horse-drawn ambulances and motor-ambulances, which are very badly wanted to convey from railway stations horses kicked and lamed en route, and horses not injured severely enough to necessitate their being destroyed, but suffering from wounds that prevent their walking to the station to the convalescent farms. Motor-lorries are needed for the rapid conveyance of fodder from the base hospitals, where the stores are kept, to the convalescent farms and hospitals miles away. With the advent of winter, the horses are unable to graze, and so there is more feeding to be done.

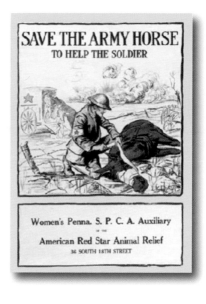

Of course the army had its own resources and while charitable support from home was no doubt welcomed, the AVC grew rapidly from an establishment of a few hundred in 1914 to 15 600 serving officers and men at the war's end, excluding Dominion veterinary personnel. While initial treatment of sick or injured animals fell on the staff of each mounted unit or infantry brigade under its veterinary officer, or by the divisional mobile veterinary section, the AVC, through eighteen veterinary hospitals established behind the lines, became the core arm in the military's treatment of horses.

Wounded horses being taken aboard a barge on a French canal for onward transport to a veterinary hospital. At the war's end the Army Veterinary Corps received the following commendation: 'The Corps by it's initiative and scientific methods has placed military veterinary organisation on a higher plane. The high standard which it has maintained at home and throughout all theatres has resulted in a reduction of animal wastage, an increased mobility of mounted units and a mitigation of animal suffering unapproached in any previous military operation.'

129

But while veterinary care was essential in keeping animals healthy, the principal role of the AVC was to return as many sick and wounded animals as rapidly as possible back to operational service. In the meantime it was left to the fighting men and their various units to work daily with their animals, to care for them up to the point where specialist treatment was required, and to keep them fed and watered.

It would also be the distressing duty of individual soldiers to despatch horse and mules that were so badly injured that shooting them was the only course of action. Putting an animal 'out of its misery' is a laudable thing but in reality it leaves a remembrance that it difficult to erase. Dr F.O. Taylor, serving in France with the RFA and the RAMC recalls the aftermath of an artillery bombardment:

> *A beautiful chestnut mare stood patiently tethered to a tree, bleeding slowly to death from a small wound in the belly, through which a flying fragment had passed; the blood dripped steadily on, and one could not think of the poor animal's final and tedious death; as I had at one time been a combatant officer I was beseeched to put an end to its misery with a rifle which was produced from somewhere. All that I can say about this is that I did it... but it is another haunting memory.*

The *Field Service Pocket Book* provides a terse and dispassionate instruction on how best to achieve this:

> *To shoot a horse – Lift up the forelock and place it under the brow band. Place muzzle of revolver almost touching the skin where the lowest hairs of the forelock grow.*

• • •

The provisioning of horses proved one of the major abiding problems of the war, both for the military leaders and the politicians. It would not be stretching credulity too far to suggest that, had the war continued beyond 1918, the issue would have been a major factor in deciding the war's outcome.

Horses were essential to the process of war, and having, by one means or another, secured the necessary thousands of animals to carry out their military objectives, the army then needed to feed them. Horses consume large amounts of food that is generally bulky and easily spoiled if subjected to rainwater or damp conditions. This means that transportation of such feedstuff is critical both in having the necessary capacity available and in the speed in which it can be delivered. Moreover, horses require oats, bran or some other grain as part of their daily intake if they are to be kept healthy, especially in trying or stressful conditions. Humans also rely on grain for bread, and as part of a cheap but wholesome diet. With a shortage of horse power and ploughmen on farms in Britain, growing enough grain to feed both horses and the general population became an increasing problem as the war years passed. Poor harvests exacerbated the problem. Rationing of foodstuffs gave rise to mutterings that horses at the front enjoyed a better diet than the people at home. The government looked abroad to procure more feedstuffs but the Germans sinking so many merchant ships added to the difficulties when it came to making a choice between importing horses (and other war material), or the food to feed them (or the people). The Ministry of Shipping, with little interest in horses, pressed the government to restrict the ship-ment of forage, which they did, in turn cutting the ration of oats and hay for horses.

By January 1918 the War Cabinet became increasingly exercised by this dilemma and shortly afterwards were obliged to introduce an order prohibiting the feeding of cereals to horses, other than those used for military or agricultural purposes. Around the same time the daily ration of oats for army horses was cut by two pounds. The fact that this released an astonishing half million additional tons of shipping starkly

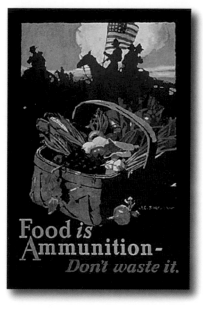

The USA played its part in reducing the pressure on available resources.

Unloading sacks of oats at a French quayside on to a train. The pressure on shipping led to the British government having to make a choice between importing food or war materials. Whether for horses or for humans, grain took up a great deal of space on merchant ships and led to arguments in the War Office over prioritising cargoes.

131

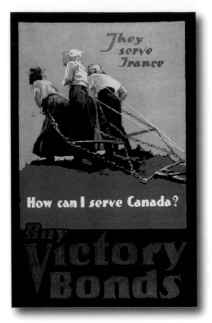

The image on the poster appeared originally on a poster in France. It shows three heroic peasant women in harness, taking the place of horses. By 1916 food shortages in Europe were having a profound affect on the progress of the war.

illustrates the huge scale involved in feeding horses at the front. This still meant that heavy horses consumed ten pounds of oats per day. At the outset of the war the daily recommendation for heavy draught army horses was 14 pounds of grain, 15 pounds of dried grass and 1 ounce of salt.

Fortunately for the government, its people and horses, by early 1918, with the USA sending even more men and material into Europe, the outcome of the war was becoming more assured. With the U Boat threat receding more shipments were reaching our shores and former ploughmen were being released from front line duty to return to work on the land.

Throughout the war, for the fighting men, providing themselves and their horses with enough food and water was a perpetual difficulty, as this cavalryman recalls during the retreat of the BEF in 1914.

The position over the rations for both men and horses was rather precarious. These were the days when we went without rations of any kind or water. The horses were more or less starved of water. On the retreat we went to various streams with our buckets, but no sooner had we got the water halfway back to them, than we moved again.

The reality of getting food to horses at the Front. In filthy conditions this rider is using a makeshift sledge to haul a bale of hay and a sack of grain to the horse lines.

We had strong feelings towards our horses. We went into the fields and beat the corn and oats out of the ears and brought them back, but that didn't save them. As the days went on, the horse's belly got more up into the middle of its back, and the cry was frequently down the line, 'Saddler – a plate and a punch!' This meant that the saddler had to come along and punch some more holes in the horse's leather girth to keep the saddles on.

For the men at the front, keeping horses watered and fed was a daily chore, made worse by the ever-present threat of attack and by the variable weather. While a horse needs only around 10–12 gallons of water per day in winter, this leaps to 20–25 gallons in summer, especially if the horse has been working hard. Finding a constant and potable source of water could mean travelling long distances, and in winter often meant having to chop through ice-bound pools.

Contrasting scenes of watering horses in winter and summer. The top photograph shows draught horses at a frozen watering hole where the pick axe indicates troops have had to break through the ice to reach the water. The lower photograph was taken in high summer, with thirsty horses drinking at a purpose-built trough.

133

A party of soldiers have been mowing a field of clover which they are loading into the lorry. Even when supplies of imported hay were plentiful at the front, fresh forage such as this would be much more nutritional.

British soldiers in France cutting bedding for their horses.

Generally men liked the time spent with horses for it provided them with an opportunity for 'normal' work in what were often trying circumstances. But in at least one instance the provision of horse feed was used as field punishment when William Howells, of the Royal Horse Artillery, having been found guilty of threatening violence to a fellow soldier, was given '28 days punishment crushing oats' for horses.

But their were lighter occasions too. In his diary Travis Hampson MC describes a delightful moment in France in 1914.

At one place where we crossed a lovely clear small river, like one of the chalk streams at home, the horses were unharnessed and ridden into the water. It was deep enough to make the drivers kneel on their backs. There was no difficulty in getting the horses in, but a good deal in getting them out, as they were enjoying it so thoroughly. I should have liked a swim myself, and don't really know why some of us didn't go in.

Watched by their comrades, troopers of the Royal Scots Greys take their horses into a French mill pool to water them.

THE WAR HORSES

The constant problem of dealing with horses' feet was set at the door of the farriers attached to division or regimental units or, when a problem became more serious, by the AVC farriers behind the lines. Some of the contrast in the two circumstances is illustrated in the photographs below.

A final thought on the care of horses by the army can be left to Colonel the Right Hon. Mark Lockwood, writing towards the end of the war in *The War Illustrated*.

Contrasting scenes between farriery undertaken at an AVC base and near the front lines. In the photograph below there appears to be an element of training underway and the general conditions are immaculate. On the right a mule stands in a set of rudimentary stocks. It is lifting a bandaged hoof suggesting the reason for its need for treatment. A large pair of bellows indicates that farriery work is done here from time to time.

Until the time comes when the Red Cross of Geneva protects human and animal combatants alike, we, who have made laws to protect animals in peace time, must take all care to protect them also in war time. The horses of the British Army are an integral part of the British Army itself, and the care which the soldiers give to their horses shows that they value their co-operation and their friendship. We all want to help the men who are fighting for their country's honour, and, having helped them to the best of our ability, we must continue to see that their horses are not neglected.

Home

The various signatures on the Armistice, signed between the Germans and the Allies in a railway carriage in the Compiegne Forest in 1918, spelt out a seismic shift between one world and another. The 16 million human deaths caused by the war worldwide was more than matched by at least 50 million (some suggest almost 100 million) who died in the Spanish Flu pandemic of 1918. A glance at any village memorial to the Great War brings the effects of the wartime casualties into a sharper perspective; the names carved there representing a startlingly high proportion of the youth of each parish: a lost generation indeed.

The men who survived to return home, many of them scarred or injured to the point of permanent infirmity, now had a different view of the world. They had been to places and seen things they simply could not communicate to their wives and families; dark secrets often. But they returned also with new skills, a new confidence and a wider view of the world that, had they never left, would have kept rural life moving at its former dawdling pace.

A sign of the times. This photograph, taken in the early 1920s, shows members of the Royal Army Service Corps on exercises on Salisbury Plain. A large tracked vehicle stands ahead of the RASC lorry in the bed of which are tethered, rather ignominiously, a quartet of horses.

At home, food shortages remained acute and rationing of foodstuffs remained in place for months after the war's end. Meat remained on ration until December 1919, butter until May 1920 and sugar in November of that year.

A child's ration book from 1919. Foodstuffs on ration included meat, bacon, butter, margarine, sugar and tea.

Soldiers returned home to families that were close to starvation. The government was under pressure to reduce the country's reliance on expensive imported food and to get British farming back on its feet. In February 1919 a Board of Agriculture and Fisheries report complained that the Department of Demobilisation and Resettlement had been dilatory in getting men back to work on the land. Those skilled in ploughing etc. had been designated as 'pivotal' men and 29 792 of these had been given priority release, but progress was slow.

At the war's end British forces were equipped with 57 000 lorries and tractors, 23 000 light road vehicles and 7000 motor ambulances. Large numbers of these became available on the open market, added to which the government's 1917 plans to import and produce more tractors resulted in a sudden bonanza of mechanical transport. Moreover, while the 'ploughmen of England' who had signed up in their millions (and died in their thousands) could not be replaced, soldier-engineers, familiar with petrol and diesel engines formed an eager workforce willing to replace them.

It would have happened in any case, but these circumstances provided a springboard from which lorries replaced horses and carts, and on the land horse power gave way to tractors. The change in agriculture came more quickly on the rich sweeping farm-lands of central England, but on poorer hill farms and among the pattern of small fields in the westcountry the horse held sway for many years. At Burnham Market in rural Norfolk the first fully mechanised harvest did not take place until 1935.

The British Army were now faced with a difficulty; what to do with the thousands of horses it owned, not only in France but across the world, but which it no longer needed. They placed their disposal in the hands of the AVC. In Europe the army had already faced the wrath of the animal welfare charities over the sale of unwanted horses to French farmers, and further disposals caused the RSPCA to threaten with-drawal of its support. There arose nationally an indignation over the idea that horses which had served Britain so well were now being sold off to the French for meat and figures suggest that at least 45 000 animals were sent for slaughter for this purpose in Europe alone.

Eventually as a result of this disapprobation the government made moves towards ensuring that, where horses were sold abroad for labour, there would be checks to ensure the purchasers were bona fide. By 1919 almost a quarter of a million horses were sold at home and abroad, raising almost £8 million, a small recovery when set against the total cost to Britain in purchasing horses throughout the duration of the war of £67.5 million.

A government poster from 1917 reminds a hungry British population of the stark choice between guns and bread. Every shipment of imported grain further reduced Britain's military capacity.

A number of horses on being repatriated were fêted as heroes. This poignant photograph is of Bill, a veteran British artillery horse who served faithfully with the 47th Battery of the Royal Field Artillery, 2nd Division from 1914–1919. In view of the wastage rates on the Western Front it was remarkable for a horse to have survived the entire campaign.

That two countries separated by a few miles of sea should have such irreconcilable views regarding the consumption of horse meat remains a mystery, but the debate as to its propriety remains today. We know that horse meat was eaten by the British in the Boer War. In the First World War did British troops, when short of food, and often in close quarters with French comrades in arms, never share their allies' meat rations? The answer appears to be no, although one soldier, Joseph Murray, recalling Christmas Day on the Somme hints otherwise.

Well, we asked for it and we got it; a good measure of potato stew, jackets included, cabbage that looked like seaweed and tasted like it, and small chunks of the aforementioned 'fresh' meat. It may have been fresh before hostilities began but it was certainly not fresh now, nor was it beef or mutton!

Figures vary widely but it appears that somewhere between 60 000 and 100 000 animals were repatriated to Britain to be sold at auction. While there was a strong initial demand for draught horses, prices dropped sharply once the immediate requirement had been fulfilled. Slowly life began to return to some kind of normality, but the full stop that was the First World War had put a firm close to the Edwardians' elegant narrative. The venerable stonework of the Establishment edifice had crumbled, never to be remade.

A pair of horses pulling a binder in a wheatfield at Bere Regis in Dorset c.1900.

The Perfection of Nature

It is almost a hundred years since the outbreak of the First World War and it would be true to say that most people in Britain today have had no first hand contact with a horse – that is to say, they have never touched a horse. A century ago the reverse would be true; most people would have ridden a horse, or would have been carried in some form of transportation pulled by horses; many would be familiar with the daily routine of feeding, mucking out and grooming, through which close contact came recognition of the different character of individual animals. Back then everyone saw, smelled or heard horses as part of their daily lives.

Over those years, as we have slowly lost communion with the natural world, our understanding, our sensitivity, towards animals has been replaced by a kind of yearning sentimentality. Such sentiments go some way towards explaining present society's demonstrative idealism in respect of the animal kingdom, particularly when it comes to our pets.

In *Gulliver's Travels* Jonathan Swift uses horses to symbolise nobility and purity, giving them the name Houyhnhnm – meaning 'the perfection of nature'. Swift's satirical aims aside, there are obvious reasons for his choice of horses, to whose kingdom Gulliver journeys: the human relationship with the horse began at the dawn of civilisation and Swift recognises the strength of the bonds that tie horse and man together, using this in his story so that we might hold a mirror up to ourselves.

Gulliver explains to the leader of the Houyhnhnm the nature of human duplicity and deceit. But the horse is a nobel and honourable animal; they have no word for lying, and can only conceive of lies as 'the thing that was not'. During their discourse on war the horse shrugs off the idea that man could exact much damage on his fellows.

For, your mouths lying flat with your faces, you can hardly bite each other to any purpose, unless by consent. Then as to the claws upon your feet before and behind, they are so short and tender... And therefore, in recounting the numbers of those who have been killed in battle, I cannot but think you have said the thing which is not.

Gulliver then explains to the horse the inexhaustible ingenuity of man in waging war.

THE WAR HORSES

And being no stranger to the art of war, I gave him a description of cannons, culverins, muskets, carabines, pistols, bullets, powder, swords, bayonets, battles, sieges, retreats, attacks, undermines, countermines, bombardments, sea fights, ships sunk with a thousand men, twenty thousand killed on each side, dying groans, limbs flying in the air, smoke, noise, confusion, trampling to death under horses' feet, flight, pursuit, victory; fields strewed with carcases, left for food to dogs and wolves and birds of prey; plundering, stripping, ravishing, burning...

Sadly the human taste for war as described by Swift shows little sign of abating, but at least we can hope that no future war will require the direct sacrifice of so many million animals as did that of 1914–18. And at this distance, a century on, how might *we* explain to some other noble beast our justification for the slaughter of the First World War?

A young horse stands over the body of the rider who, even in death, clutches the reins of his mount.

BIBLIOGRAPHY

The principal documents and publications referred to in research for this book are in the author's collection, these and other selected titles are listed here.

Arthur, Max. *Forgotten Voices of the Great War*. Ebury Press, London 2002

Beaver, Patrick (Ed.) *The Wipers Times*. Peter Davis, London 1973

Bergonzi, Bernard. *Heroes Twilight*. Constable, London 1980

Blunden, Edmund. *Undertones of War*. William Collins & Sons, Glasgow 1965.

Bond, Alan (Ed.). *The Martial Muse*. Wheaton, Exeter 1976

Bone, Sir Muirhead. *War Drawings*. George Newnes Ltd, London 1917

Brooke, Rupert. *The Complete Poems*. Sidgwick & Jackson, London 1952

Buchan, John. *Nelson's History of the War. Vol 1–24*. Thomas Nelson, London 1915–1919

Cassidy, Michael. *Sapper's War Stories*. Hodder & Stoughton, London, 1930

Churchill, Winston. *The World Crisis 1914–1918*. Butterworth, London 1931

Clarke, Alan. *The Donkeys*. Hutchinson, London 1961

Downes, Alison & Childs, Alan. *My Life with Horses*. Halsgrove, 2006

Ellis, John. *Eye-Deep in Hell. The Western Front 1914–18*. Croom Helm Ltd, London 1976

Evans, George Ewart. *Horse Power and Magic*. Faber & Faber, London 1979.

Evans, Martin Marix. *Over the Top. Great Battles of the First World War*. Arcturus Publishing, London 2002

Evans, Martin Marix. *1918. The Year of Victories*. Arcturus Publishing, London 2002

Ewart, Wildred et al. *Fifty Amazing Stories of the Great War*. Odhams Press Ltd, London 1936

Falls, Cyril. *The First World War*. Longmans Green & Co. London 1960.

French, Field Marshal John, *1914*. Constable & Co., London 1919

Fussell, Paul. *The Great War and Modern Memory*. Oxford University Press, 1975

Gardner, Brian. *Up the Line to Death*. Methuen, London 1969

Gerard, James W. *Face to Face with Kaiserism*. Hodder & Stoughton, London 1918

Gibbs, Philip. *The War Dispatches*. Phillips Ltd 1964

Graves, Robert. *Goodbye to All That*. Jonathan Cape, London 1929

Grimshaw, Captain Roly. *Indian Cavalry Officer 1915–15*. Costello, Kent 1986

Harrie, Meirion & Susie. *The War Artists*. Michael Jospeh, 1983.

Hart, Edward. *The Suffolk Punch*. Halsgrove, 2007

Hastings, Max. *The Oxford Book of Military Anecdotes*. Oxford University Press, 1985

Hesketh-Pritchard, Major H. *Sniping in France*. Hutchinson, London 1920

Hocking, Joseph. *Tommy*. Hodder & Stoughton nd

Innes, T.A. & Castle, Ivor. *Covenants With Death*. Daily Express Publications, London 1934

Johnson, Peter. *Front Line Artists*. Cassell, London 1978.

Jones, D.L. (Ed.). *War Poetry: An Anthology*. Pergamon Press, Oxford 1968

Keegan, John. *The American Civil War*. Hutchinson, London 2009

Keegan, John. *The First World War. An Illustrated History*. Hutchinson, London 2001

Kenyon, David. *British Cavalry on the Western Front 1916–1918*, unpublished thesis, 2007

King Albert's Book. Hodder & Stoughton, London 1914

Lewis, Cecil. *Sagittarius Rising*. Peter Davis, London 1936

Liddell Hart, B.H. *History of the First World War*. Cassell & Co., London 1970.

Liddle, Peter H. *Home Fires and Foreign Fields*. Brasseys Defence Publishers, London 1985

Lloyd George, David. *War Memoirs*. Odhams Press, London 1938

Lobban, Robin. *The First World War*. Oxford University Press, 1982

Lord Roberts Memorial Fund Stamp Album. Fawcett & Co, London 1915

MacGill, Patrick. *The Great Push*. Herbert Jenkins, London 1916

Marshall-Cornwall, James. *Haig as Military Commander*. Batsford, 1973

Masefield, John. *Gallipoli*. Heinemann, London 1916

Masefield, John. *The Old Front Line*. Heinemann, London 1917

Mayhew, Henry. *Mayhew's London* (Ed. Peter Quennell). Spring Books, New York 1969

Maurice, Sir F. *Forty Days in 1914*. Constable & Co., London 1919

McCrae, John. *In Flanders Fields*. Hodder & Stoughton, London 1919

Mottistone, Lord (General Jack Seely. *My Horse Warrior*. Hodder & Stoughton, London 1934

Mumby, Frank A. (Ed.) *The Great World War: A History Vols 1–9*. Gresham Publishing Co., London 1927

Murray, Joseph. *Call to Arms*. William Kimber, London 1980

O'Neill, H.C. *A History of the War*. T.C. & E.C. Jack, London 1920.

O'Rorke, B.G. *In the Hands of the Enemy*. Longmans Green & Co. London 1916.

Parliamentary Papers 1900–1924, various digitised records. www.parliament.co.uk

Punch. *Mr Punch's History of the Great War*. Cassell, 1918

Remarque, Erich Maria. *All Quiet on the Western Front*. Heinemann, London 1970

Russell, Arthur. *The Machine Gunner*. Roundwood Press, 1977

Sassoon, Siegfried. *Memoirs of a Fox Hunting Man*. Faber & Faber, London 1936

Sassoon, Siegfried. *Memoirs of an Infantry Officer*. Faber & Faber, London 1930

Service, Robert W. *The Rhymes of a Red Cross Man*. T. Fisher Unwin Ltd, 1916

Sherriff R.C. & Bartlett Vernon. *Journey's End*. Gollancz 1930

Swift, Jonathan. *Gulliver's Travels*. Spencer Press, London 1937

Terraine, John. *White Heat. The New Warfare 1914–1918*. Guild Publishing 1982

Titler, Dale M. *The Day the Red Baron Died*. Ian Allan, London 1973

Turner P.W. & Haigh, R.H. (Eds) *Not for Glory*. Robert Maxwell, London 1969

Turner P.W. & Haigh, R.H. (Eds) *The Long Carry*. Pergamon Press, Oxford 1970

Vansittart, Peter. *Voices from the Great War*. Jonathan Cape, London 1981

Various. *History of the First World War. Vols 1–8*. Purnell, BPC Publishing, London nd

War Office. *Field Service Pocket Book*. London, 1914.

Winter, Dennis. *Death's Men. Soldiers of the Great War*. Penguin, London 1978

Winter, Jay & Baggett, Blaine. *1914–1918*. BBC Books, 1996

Wolff, Leon. *In Flanders Fields*. Penguin Books, London 1979